To be intentional is to do something on purpose, and that is the vision laid before you in this book. Practical, doable, affordable ideas are shared to inspire you to be more purposeful as a parent, spouse, and child of God in ways that will inspire your kids to be purposeful and intentional in all they do as well.

Joey and Carla Link
Award-winning authors of *Taming the Lecture*
Bug and Getting Your Kids to Think
Founders, Parenting Made Practical

This book is a breath of fresh air for those who long to have healthy families. It is an intentional roadmap toward building vibrant, fun, and Jesus-centered families. You will find practical tips for parenting and marriage that you can apply every day. Better yet, spend time with the Corbin family and you will see firsthand how they live this out!

Jim Brown
Lead Pastor, Grace Community Church

By God's design, the family is where kids are meant to find a place to belong and grow into themselves. But in our fast-paced world, we have lost the intentionality and space needed to foster our kids' confidence. In this reflective book, Anastasia highlights the importance of becoming an intentional family. But she doesn't stop there. With practical examples, reflective questions, and applications, she invites parents to heal from their own past and create for their family a better future.

Micah Ruth
Author of *You Are Loved & Free*, speaker, homeschool mom

Becoming an Intentional Family is authentic, fresh, and full of great ideas to help jump-start or continue ways to connect your family members and make your relationships a priority. Anastasia has a beautiful gift for merging life experiences with creative suggestions to help guide your focus on what matters most to you. All of those who are looking for growth in their family dynamics will find this a beneficial read.

Natalie Replogle
Author of *Come to My Rescue* book series
Coauthor of the mom's devotional, *When the Bases are Loaded*
Women's Ministry Director, Grace Community Church

The Christian family faces challenges daily as the world tries its best to conform our children to its standards. In *Becoming an Intentional Family*, Anastasia offers practical advice on creating memories and building confidence in your children. Now more than ever, our children need to know they are loved and valued. This book explores the aspects of family, marriage, parenting, home, and outreach through journaling prompts, prayer, and scripture. So pack your backpack and enjoy creating some fantastic memories with your family!

Missy Eversole
Author, *Transformed, Not Conformed: Embracing a Life-Changing Approach to Spiritual Habits*

BECOMING AN
INTENTIONAL
FAMILY

BECOMING AN INTENTIONAL
FAMILY

CREATING MEANINGFUL MEMORIES
AND BUILDING CONFIDENCE
IN YOUR KIDS

ANASTASIA CORBIN

Anastasia Corbin
Zephaniah 3:17

Published by Redemption Press, PO Box 427, Enumclaw, WA 98022.
Toll-Free (844) 2REDEEM (273-3336)

Redemption Press is honored to present this title in partnership with the author. The views expressed or implied in this work are those of the author. Redemption Press provides our imprint seal representing design excellence, creative content, and high-quality production.

The author has tried to recreate events, locales, and conversations from memories of them. In order to maintain their anonymity, in some instances the names of individuals, some identifying characteristics, and some details may have been changed, such as physical properties, occupations, and places of residence.

ISBN 13: 978-1-64645-389-4 (Paperback)
978-1-64645-391-7 (ePub)
978-1-64645-390-0 (Mobi)

Library of Congress Catalog Card Number: 2022910167

Dedication

To my four kids: Micaela, Nathan, Analiah, and Caleb. One of my greatest joys in life is being your mom. My prayer is for you to have a deep relationship with God and know without a doubt that you are fully known and loved by Him.

Contents

Acknowledgments

First and foremost, to Jesus, my Lord and Savior—words cannot express my gratitude to You. Thank you for choosing me and bringing me out of darkness into light. Thank you for all that you went through for me so that I may have abundant life. I love you, and my heart's cry is to honor You in all that I do. May You alone be glorified through this book.

Jonathan, thank you for always supporting me and encouraging me to go after what God has called me to do. Writing this book would not have been possible without your love and support. Thanks for believing in me.

Micaela, Nathan, Analiah, and Caleb, I love being your mom! Thank you for your love, patience, and grace for me. Thank you for your forgiveness for the many times I mess up. Your encouragement and support on the journey to write this book were also a blessing.

Megan, Jewel, Tara, Natalie and Angela, your friendship is a true blessing. Thanks for always pointing me to Jesus. Thanks for believing in me and pushing me when I wanted to give up. Your encouragement means more than you'll ever know.

The Becoming an Intentional Family Prayer Warrior Team: Erica, Ginger, Janette, Angela, Bobbie, Dana, Heath, Lael, Kathy, Tiffany, Missy, Juli, Catherine, Kalie, Tiffany, Shelly, Sharon, Ginny, Barb, Kristi, Aimee, Tara, Natalie, Megan, Jewel, Anne, and Keri, you are all a treasure. Thank you for the countless prayers on my behalf. It was a blessing to know I could share anything and have so many people praying. Love each of you! A heartfelt thank-you to Tara, Natalie, Megan, Jewel, Anne, and Keri, who have been with me from the beginning of this journey.

Lou Erste and Mary Burke, thank you for being my Dad and Mom. Having children of my own gives me a deeper appreciation of all you did as my parents. I love you both.

Tom and Jeanne Corbin, my in-laws, thank you for praying for me even before you knew my name. Thank you also for your legacy of commitment to one another and more importantly to God. I love and appreciate you both.

Christi Miller, thank you so much for your expertise as an editor. You pushed me and challenged me in so many ways, and I am so grateful. This book would not be what it is without you. Thank you for your encouragement and for believing in me.

Kim, Jan, Miranda, Tammy, Dad and Michelle, Micah, Tom and Jeanne, Janette, Cindy, Sarah, Jewel, Missy, Jamie, Megan, and Keri, thank you for believing in the mission of this book. Your support means more than you know. I have asked God to bless you tenfold. Thank you also to everyone who gave toward the audio book project. I also asked God to bless you tenfold.

Melody and Greg of The Limberlost Place, thank you for providing a peaceful and quiet setting to write my book. You are such a blessing to me!

Angela Driskell and Journey Websites, thank you for your hard work with my Creating Meaningful Memories logo and website. You are all amazing and I appreciate you so much.

Main Street Coffeehouse, thank you for providing a wonderful, quiet place to write my book. Thank you also for your amazing salads!

Thank you to the team at Redemption Press! It has been a journey to get to this point, and I am so grateful to have you all at my side. Thanks for believing in the message of this book. A special thanks goes to Carrie, Hannah, and Mari for being amazing project managers and for their patience with me.

Longing to Belong

———◦———

You made all the delicate, inner parts of my body and knit me together in my mother's womb. Thank you for making me so wonderfully complex! Your workmanship is marvelous—how well I know it.

Psalm 139:13–14

I've never met a child who didn't long to be noticed. I wrote this book for every child who has ever wanted to fit in with all the other kids.

This child wants to be seen, known, and accepted for who they are. This child is part of a family but doesn't feel they have a place to belong. This child longs to be understood and valued by their family.

I am that child. Maybe you are that child. As you read this book, you will learn that you are fully known and loved by God. You do belong. You are important and valuable even if you have been told otherwise.

———◦———

It was the summer after my seventh-grade school year. My siblings and I were invited to my sister's friend's pool for the afternoon. The cool water felt so good on this hot and humid day. After we swam for a while, a neighborhood kid showed up. That's when things started to go downhill for me.

He singled me out and called me the N-word and made fun of me because my skin was so dark. That summer, I had tanned really well, so I did

13

look African American. It helped that my oldest brother had words with this kid, but it didn't ease the deep ache in my heart. The afternoon was ruined for me. Swimming wasn't fun anymore. I just wanted to go home.

Later that afternoon, tears ran down my face, the pain cutting deep. Why didn't I fit in? Why was my skin so dark? I just wanted to belong somewhere.

Dirty Knees

My knees have been well washed. Sometimes I scrubbed them so hard, they ached. Why did I scrub my knees? I wanted to look like everyone else. I longed to fit in.

I inherited my Mexican genes from my great-grandfather. My skin tone is olive all year. Because of that, my knees are darker. As a child, I honestly believed I could scrub my knees and make them look like my friends' knees. Later in life, I realized what a gift my skin tone was.

As one of eight children, I easily got lost in the shuffle during my growing-up years. My parents did the best they could with what they knew. I wanted my parents' attention, but I didn't get enough of it. I remember deciding that when I had children one day, I would work hard to give all of them attention.

In our large family, we never had a dull moment. Something was always going on. We had the normal sibling fights and arguments with our parents. My parents' relationship was always unstable, and I often wondered if it was my fault. I wasn't necessarily a kid who got into a lot of trouble, but I did act out, so I wondered if my behavior caused my parents to split. For a while, I wanted to help them fix their marriage, but eventually I started praying for them to get a divorce.

Even though I prayed this way, I felt guilty for wanting it. I also had a lot of stomachaches as a kid. I told my mom about the stomachaches, but nothing was ever resolved. I just toughed it out, and soon it began to feel normal. Now I realize a lot of it had to do with the tension in our home.

My parents married at the age of eighteen and had a rocky start. Once they started having babies, their problems escalated. My dad worked long hours, leaving my mom to care for us all without much support. When my parents did talk, they often yelled and screamed. As kids, we hid in our bedrooms and covered our ears. Or we talked to one another and tried to get our minds off our parents' yelling.

I questioned whether I was loved. I often said "I love you" to my parents, hoping they would return the sentiment. I didn't hear those words from them until my senior year of high school. I clearly remember being at my boyfriend's house and calling my mom to let her know I was getting home later. I held my breath and ended the call with "I love you, Mom." When she said "I love you too," tears welled up in my eyes.

Throughout my childhood, I wondered what was wrong with me. Why couldn't I be accepted and loved? I grew up with a lot of unrest, anxiety, and fear. In my high school years, I tried to fill my void by dating boys who showed me love and affection. Now I know that is not what God intended for me.

When I met Jesus in college, I realized my worth and value was in Him. I grew up in the Catholic church, so I knew all the stories about God. I knew that Jesus died on the cross for me. I was also taught that I needed to earn my way to heaven. I never met anyone who wasn't Catholic until I went to college.

Then, during my freshman year of college, I met the girls on my floor.

My roommate, Amy, and floormate Christy were the ones who talked to me about Jesus the most. They helped me to see that the only way to heaven was by accepting Jesus as my Lord and Savior. He did the work on the cross to save me. I didn't need to earn my way to heaven, nor could I. I just needed to accept this free gift of salvation. I asked Jesus to be the Lord and Savior of my life in September of 1996.

Amy taught me what devotion time was, and she told me I could have my own Bible. She taught me how to dig into God's Word and encouraged me to go to it any time I needed help. I am so thankful that Amy and Christy took time to speak into my life and tell me about Jesus. Literally, I am forever changed and grateful.

In a lot of ways, I am still learning that my worth and value are in Jesus. When my husband, Jonathan, and I got married, I wanted our kids to grow up in a home where they knew without a shadow of a doubt that they were loved, wanted, and valued. I knew this would be a process, since I had a lot to learn about parenting.

Jonathan's family modeled love and acceptance in many ways. I felt very wanted and valued right away in his family. I am also a people watcher, so whenever I noticed a confident child at our church, I studied their family and the ways they interacted. In our early years of marriage, Jonathan and I both read a lot of books about family life and parenting. I wanted to glean as much information as I could.

I also knew it was worth whatever effort it would take. Children need a place to belong and a family to belong to. It reminds me of the African proverb that states, "You want to go fast, go alone. You want to go far, go together." Children are on a journey in life, but they can't do it alone. As parents, we need to help our kids know they have a place where they belong.

Jonathan and I have been parents for sixteen years now. Our oldest daughter, Micaela, is sixteen, our son Nathan is fourteen, our daughter Analiah is eleven, and our son Caleb is nine. We live in northern Indiana. On an average evening, you will find Jonathan and me attending a cross-country meet or a football, volleyball, soccer, or basketball game. We often divide and conquer because at least three of our kids are involved in sports at one time. It's a full season but one I would never trade.

During the day you will find Jonathan hanging in a tree—literally. He is a tree trimmer, and for the past fifteen years, he has spent most of his days sixty to ninety feet in the air. Jonathan is also a business coach. He loves to help small-business owners see their potential and succeed in what God has called them to do.

I taught second and sixth grade for six years before Micaela was born. Since then, I have been a stay-at-home mom. In 2015, I started a blog and have been writing ever since. My days are filled with reading, writing, household duties, and cuddling with our cute cockapoo puppy, Bentley. We call him my fifth kid. In addition, I help Jonathan with the tree business by running errands and doing random jobs for him. I have done some side work for a friend who owns a website design business. At least once a month, you will find me singing on the worship team at our church. I love praising God with a community of believers and leading in worship.

So, there is a little about me. You also need to know that I have a passion for people to feel they belong. This book is a result of that passion. Jonathan jokes about how much I reach out to random people. The Holy Spirit will prompt me to talk to people I haven't met and invite them to our small group. I also invite new friends, especially people who are new to our church, to meet me for coffee. I want them to know they are seen and that they are fully known and deeply loved by God.

Jonathan and I have learned so much along the way and continue to grow in our parenting and marriage. Our parenting plays a part in helping our children feel they belong, but it's not the only part. We have found that our marriage relationship, the time we spend together as a family, the environment of our home, and being on mission are all part of the bigger picture. We cannot become an intentional family without each part.

We incorporate our time together as a family into our parenting. But we also spend time getting to know each other as a family group, laughing together, and enjoying each other. As you will read in Part Three, we need to know our children personally and learn ways to enjoy their specific makeup.

Becoming an Intentional Family will dig into these five aspects of an intentional family: family, marriage, parenting, home, and outreach. This book will be a resource along the journey as you learn to give your children the gift of belonging. It is a combination of ideas to help shape your family and give your children a place to belong. The ideas will also help you in your journey as you create meaningful memories and build confidence in your kids.

Knowing what to pack for any journey can be a challenge, with countless items to remember. The best way to pack for a trip is to make a list: passport, clothes, socks, deodorant, walking shoes, and camera.

Of course, every journey is different, so the items we pack depend on the journey. If you are reading this book, you're probably on a journey with your family, and you want a positive, loving, and impactful experience.

Perhaps you have stalled in your journey. Maybe you're almost ready to give up and need encouragement. Or maybe you already live intentionally and want to learn more.

We are all at different points in our family journeys. Each family has room to grow. This book is meant to guide you in your journey toward becoming an intentional family and giving your children the gift of belonging.

Intentional Family

Think back to all your good childhood memories. What circumstances surrounded those memories? Was it a special trip or going for ice cream with your mom? Do these memories bring a smile to your face?

An intentional family creates time in their schedule to make these kinds of special, lasting memories. Children often remember outings with just Mom or Dad and vacations to the same place each year. The purpose of an intentional family is to build a stronger bond so children feel loved and valued and know they have a place of belonging.

If your desire is to create meaningful family memories and a place for your children to belong, then I invite you to come along on the journey. *Becoming an Intentional Family* will guide you. Each part of the book will share some packing items for your Intentional Backpack to help you create family identity. At the end of each chapter, there are action steps to choose from and a Bible verse or verses related to the topic of the chapter. . After reading those verses, study questions are provided to help you go deeper. There is also a gentle challenge, encouragement, and a prayer to read. Next, lines are provided to write your own prayer. There is also extra journaling space for you to make note of anything you want to remember from the chapter.

Choose the items you want to pack, and reference this book as a checklist at any time. Are you ready? Let's go!

O Lord, you have examined my heart
and know everything about me.
You know when I sit down or stand up.
You know my thoughts even when I'm far away.
You see me when I travel
and when I rest at home.

You know everything I do.
You know what I am going to say.
You go before me and follow me.
You place your hand of blessing on my head.
Such knowledge is too wonderful for me,
too great for me to understand!
I can never escape from your Spirit!
I can never get away from your presence!
If I go up to heaven, you are there;
if I go down to the grave, you are there.
If I ride the wings of the morning,
if I dwell by the farthest oceans,
even there your hand will guide me,
and your strength will support me.
I could ask the darkness to hide me
and the light around me to become night—
but even in darkness I cannot hide from you.
To you the night shines as bright as day.
Darkness and light are the same to you.
You made all the delicate, inner parts of my body
and knit me together in my mother's womb.
Thank you for making me so wonderfully complex!
Your workmanship is marvelous—how well I know it.
You watched me as I was being formed in utter seclusion,
as I was woven together in the dark of the womb.
You saw me before I was born.
Every day of my life was recorded in your book.
Every moment was laid out
before a single day had passed.
How precious are your thoughts about me, O God.
They cannot be numbered!
I can't even count them;
they outnumber the grains of sand!

And when I wake up,
you are still with me!
O God, if only you would destroy the wicked!
Get out of my life, you murderers!
They blaspheme you;
your enemies misuse your name.
O LORD, shouldn't I hate those who hate you?
Shouldn't I despise those who oppose you?
Yes, I hate them with total hatred,
for your enemies are my enemies.
Search me, O God, and know my heart;
test me and know my anxious thoughts.
Point out anything in me that offends you,
and lead me along the path of everlasting life.
(Psalm 139)

Psalm 139 is a powerful reminder of how much God knows and loves us. Even before we were born, God knew us. He knit us together in our mother's womb. He made us specifically and intentionally to be who we are. In God, we belong. As parents, we have the awesome privilege to teach our kids how much God knows and loves them.

***

Thank you for making me so wonderfully complex! Your workmanship is marvelous—how well I know it. (Psalm 139:14)

Please read Psalm 139 again, from the beginning to the end. Before reading, ask the Holy Spirit to speak to you in powerful ways. After reading the psalm, please answer the study questions below.

1. Do you feel comforted by the fact that God knows everything about you? Why or why not?

_____

_____

_____

2. Have you ever hidden from God? If so, why?

_____

_____

_____

3. What was it like when you stopped hiding from God?

_____

_____

_____

4. Name a few ways God has guided you in your life.

_____

_____

_____

5. You are wonderfully made. Do you believe that? If so, name one way you live this out. If you don't believe it, please pause right now and ask the Holy Spirit to help you believe it.

_____

_____

_____

Gentle Challenge

If your desire is to create meaningful family memories and a place for your children to belong, I invite you to come along on the journey. What do you need to let go of to join me on this journey?

_____

_____

_____

Encouragement

I know it's hard to let go of the things that weigh us down. We might need to give up unrealistic expectations of ourselves or someone else's expectations of us. With God's strength, you can become the intentional parent God has called you to be.

Let's Pray

Dear God, thank you for this journey I am about to begin. Thank you that I am not alone. You go before me and follow me (Psalm 139:5), and I take great comfort in that truth. Please open my eyes and ears to all you want to teach me. Thank you, Lord. In Jesus' name, amen.

Please write your own prayer here:

_____

_____

_____

_____

Journal

_____

_____

_____

_____

_____

_____

_____

_____

_____

_____

_____

_____

_____

PART ONE

———◈———

Family: Ways to Come Together

CHAPTER 1
Gathering Your Family

———◆———

*Let us think of ways to motivate one another to acts of love and
good works. And let us not neglect our meeting together, as some
people do, but encourage one another, especially now that the
day of his return is drawing near.*
Hebrews 10:24–25

I love people watching. You can tell a lot about a person by watching them
for a few minutes. One evening, Jonathan and I were out at a restaurant
for our weekly date night. As I looked around, one family caught my eye.
I instantly brightened, and excitement coursed through me. This family
was out together during the week. They were making time to pour into
each other.

"Aww, that's so sweet. Look at the family over there!" I said. "What
a great way to connect, right?"

Moments later, every family member, even the preteens, pulled out
their devices and looked down at them.

My heart sank as I thought about the loss of connection. In today's
world, we can appear connected with many "friends" on social media. But
often, we're not connected to the people right in front of us. Don't get me
wrong. I love cell phones and think they're a great tool. But when families
use them in place of true connection, I feel sad. I long for families to gather
and connect.

Gather is a fun word. I tend to think of a mother hen gathering her chicks under her wings. It's a sweet picture, isn't it? In this chapter we'll look at ways to gather the members of your family.

We gather to build healthy relationships within our family. This helps us to learn to interact with others. When we gather, we learn healthy communication patterns, how to work with others, and ways to deal with conflict. We also learn how to react when things don't go our way.

For example, when our family plays a game together, generally one person wins the game. Often, the other kids are not happy about their sibling's win. This is a great opportunity to teach them how to cheer for others. It also teaches our kids to work through their disappointment of losing, because that is a valid feeling.

Over the years, our family has grown communication-wise. We know these life skills help them succeed in school and in their friendships. When we gather, we reflect the early church in the books of Acts.

> They worshiped together at the Temple each day, met in homes for the Lord's Supper, and shared their meals with great joy and generosity—all the while praising God and enjoying the goodwill of all the people. And each day the Lord added to their fellowship those who were being saved. (Acts 2:46–47)

Each individual family is intended to function as a mini church. We are here to serve one another, encourage each other in our walks with the Lord, and serve together. The purpose of gathering our family is to build each other up and point us toward Jesus. What a beautiful way to represent Christ to this world.

Under each section of this chapter, I will explain ways to come together. Choose the items you want to add to your Intentional Backpack.

Family Fun Nights

One way to gather is with family fun nights. There are many ways to have family fun nights. Movie night at home is easy: sit on a picnic blanket and enjoy some popcorn. You can even serve some movie theater candy boxes. Another fun night is throwing a Frisbee together at a nearby park. Another fun idea is to do a photo scavenger hunt together or split into teams if your family is larger. The winner of the scavenger hunt gets a fun prize.

Why should you make family fun nights a priority? These nights are a way to connect, have fun together, and create a stronger family bond. Children feel as if they have a place to belong in a family that laughs together and enjoys one another.

We enjoy a family fun night once a week. It is generally on Fridays but will change occasionally due to our schedule. Weekly family fun nights help to build consistency. Our kids know they can count on—and look forward to—a night together.

Family fun nights can be as simple or as involved as you like. I encourage you to add a line to your budget for these nights so you have the freedom to do what you'd like, whether it's going to the zoo, out for ice cream, or to a movie.

When our kids were younger, Jonathan and I planned the family fun nights. We spent most of them at parks around our town. We also went to splash pads in the summer. When our children turned five, we began to involve them in planning family fun nights. Now they each plan one family fun night a month. It is always interesting to see what they come up with. Here are some ideas our family enjoys:

Board Games

We all have board games buried in the closet, but how often do we use them? Dust them off and have a game night! With younger kids, Candyland and Chutes & Ladders may be your go-to games. As they get older, you'll have more variety. Our current favorite is Telestrations. Our younger two team up with Jonathan and me if the game is geared toward older kids, such as Ticket to Ride. It's a great way for us all to be involved.

This past month, each of our kids had a turn picking a board game. At the end of the month, we voted on the best game. The person who chose the winning game earned a cookie from a local bakery. Alternately, the child whose game is deemed best gets to pick out a new game for the family.

Bike Rides

Pull out the bikes and head to a nearby trail. Or you can just bike around your neighborhood. When the kids were younger, we used a bike trailer. Now, they ride on their own, which has been an adventure.

Speaking of adventures, get creative with the places you ride. One summer day, we went on an adventure to the moon. I called the kids together and asked them to get their rockets (bikes) and put on their helmets. I told them we were going to the moon.

At the time, a section of our subdivision had only a couple of houses. The center of this area was overgrown grass. I called this the moon. We rode our bikes and stopped once we arrived at the moon. I talked about what the moon was like, and then we decided to ride around the moon. We went on this adventure eight years ago, and my kids still ask to take a bike ride to the moon.

Parks and Playgrounds

Look for a nearby park or school playground. We enjoy the variety of playgrounds and parks near our home. Feel free to invite another family to come with you. It's a great way to get to know others.

Parks offer endless activities beyond playing on the playground. On a windy day, take along a kite to fly. Kids love to watch the wind blow the kite. Create or find a playground scavenger hunt sheet to do together.

Feel free to take along a football or kickball. Tag is also a fun game to play with your family. Another option is a picnic supper at the park.

Often, you will find other families at the park. This is a great opportunity to reach out and connect with new people. In your conversation, ask simple questions to get to know them. Eventually, ask the family if they attend a church. If they don't, invite them to yours. Park time can turn into outreach time.

Family Devotions

Another packing item to add to your Intentional Backpack is family devotions. This involves reading and studying God's Word together. We can turn to God's Word any time we need help or direction. It's important to train kids early about the importance of being in God's Word, corporately and individually.

When our kids were younger, we read to them from *The Beginner's Bible*. When our kids were older, we used *The Complete Illustrated Children's Bible* by Janice Emerson. After reading the Bible story, we ask questions, such as:

- What did you learn about God in this story?
- What did you learn about a Bible character?
- What can you change in your life as a result of hearing this story?

Another item to pack in your Intentional Backpack is morning devotions. We pray together and ask God to forgive us for the ways we have broken His rules. Next, we pray on the armor of God and have a time of worship. Currently, we are using *Heroes of the Bible Devotional* by Joshua Cooley. When the kids were younger, we used *The One Year Devotions for Preschoolers* by Crystal Bowman and Elena Kucharik.

Family devotions are an effective way to introduce your children to God's Word. Find a Bible that works well with whatever season of parenting you are in. Begin with one night of devotions every week, and slowly increase. You can use this same strategy with morning devotions. We enjoy using a devotional book, but you don't have to do that. You can simply read a few verses of Scripture and ask the questions above to help your children reflect on the Bible reading.

Now that our kids are older, we have family devotions differently. Each of us has our own Bible reading plan. Then, after dinner or later in the evening, we come together and share what we learned from our personal reading time.

We ask the kids to share a Scripture verse that stood out to them, tell the family why it stood out, and decide how they will apply it to their lives. This is a great way to learn what it means to apply Scripture in our daily lives. I enjoy hearing what each of our children has learned. I also love sharing what I am learning in my personal Bible study time.

Family Vacations

Family vacations are also a great item to put into your Intentional Backpack. The time with family is focused, since you are away from home, work, school, and other responsibilities, and you can have quality time to get to know one another better.

Vacations can be short or extended, depending on your season of life. One of our favorite vacations was to a friend's beach house in Michigan. It felt good to get away from the hustle of summer. Our church holds a sports camp the week before our vacation. It's a fun week of camp, but we can't connect as much as a family. Once we arrived at our friend's beach house, we fully relaxed and enjoyed being together. I absolutely love being around water, so any vacation that involves water is a win for me. The kids loved playing on the beach all day. It was a special time together.

What vacations have you enjoyed? Get creative or ask others for family vacation ideas. Pick a spot as a family. Decide what time of year you'll go, and figure the cost. Then create a goal chart as you save the amount for the trip. Kids love to see a visual, and it gives the family something to work toward.

Another option is to create a savings jar. Family members can add spare change or do extra jobs around the house to earn money. Get grandparents and other family involved in providing extra jobs for the kids to earn money.

If you are a single mom, vacations are still possible. Consider traveling with another single mom. An Airbnb is a great option. Sometimes you can find an Airbnb close to your hometown so you don't have to travel far. Or you could go to a national park. They typically have campsites or cabins. One more vacation idea is going to an all-inclusive resort. This would be a nice break for you, since the food is included.

One day I asked my Facebook friends to tell me their favorite family vacations. It was fun to read the responses. In fact, I felt excitement as I thought about the different trips my family and I could take someday. I felt the joy in my friends' hearts as they shared these precious family memories. Here are some of the responses. Maybe it will help spark an idea or two for your next family vacation.

Lindsey: I'll never forget our family road trip out west. We camped and went to Yellowstone National Park, Grand Tetons, and Mount Rushmore. My brothers and I were elementary/middle-school age. Being out in nature with family makes for lots of great memories and God moments.

Kristi: Our unanimous favorite was Clearwater Beach, Florida, where our five family members rented a cottage close to the beach and just enjoyed the beach all week. It was relaxing, and we loved the water and sand. We stayed within walking distance of stores, restaurants, and miles of beaches to walk and collect seashells. Within driving distance was the aquarium where *Dolphin Tale* was filmed, plus Disney and lots of other fun places.

Melissa: One of our family favorites was Wisconsin Dells. There we found water parks, mini golf, a mini amusement park, water shows, Ducks to ride (land/water vehicles), go-karts, tourist shops, and the list goes on. On the way there, we always stop at the Jelly Belly factory, where we get to sample their candies. Plus, they take you on a mini-tram tour to see how they make the jelly beans.

Angel: One of my favorites was the time my dad took my sister and me to Missouri. We headed west and stopped at different historic places as we saw them, including Lincoln's tomb, Jesse James's hideout (caves), and a veterans' memorial. The spontaneity was fun.

Family Dinners

One of my favorite memories as a child was sitting around the dinner table. I still remember conversation flowing and great food passing from hand to hand. The dinner table was the one place that gave me a sense of belonging as a child.

As an adult with a family of my own, I still love family dinners. We are all together, connecting in ways we can't during the day. The kids get to talk with Daddy, who is home from work. Family dinners are another item to add to your Intentional Backpack.

Jonathan and I love to use this time to hear about our kids' days. It's also a great time to teach table manners. When they go to someone else's home for dinner, we love knowing they'll behave politely at the table. Our kids also learn to serve others when we have another family over for dinner.

Research shows that regular family dinners help lower risks of smoking, drug use, eating disorders, and sexual activity. School-age children who experience a regular family dinner are also more likely to succeed in school.

Implementing Dinners

With busy schedules and hefty to-do lists, how do we implement family dinners? The key is creating time in your schedule. Start with one day a week, such as Sunday. Generally, children don't have activities and parents don't have commitments on Sundays. If you happen to have church in the evening on Sundays, I would recommend having the family dinner at lunchtime. Feel free to have your family meal after Sunday-morning church if your family prefers that. Set a time to meet at the dining room table.

Make a simple meal or serve leftovers. You can also get takeout or have a pizza delivered. The key is being together, not stressing over cooking a gourmet meal.

Once you are all gathered, start with prayer. My husband usually prays by thanking God and asking Him to bless our food. The kids are old enough now that we also ask them to take turns saying the prayer. I love hearing their simple, heartfelt prayers. For example, Caleb, our nine-year-old, prayed the other day, "Thank you, God, for our food and the fun time we had swimming today. Amen."

After prayer, use this time to get to know each other by asking questions about one another's day. We love to share highs and lows with one another. Go around the table and ask each person to answer these questions:

- What was your high today? (the part you liked the best)
- What was your low today? (a part you didn't like)
- What made you smile today?
- Who did you sit with at lunch today?
- If you could switch seats with anyone in class, who would it be and why?
- How were you brave today?

- What is one thing you learned today?
- In what way were you kind to someone today?
- If you could change one thing about your day, what would it be?

To implement these family dinners, start by having them one day a week, then slowly increase to every other day. Eventually have a family dinner every day, if possible.

Each season of life will look different though. This past fall, we had three kids in sports. The older two kids didn't get home until after one went to his football practice, so I often connected with the younger two kids while they ate an early dinner. Later, I sat down again with the rest of the family to eat dinner together.

If you can't meet for dinner as a whole family, try to make time to connect each evening after everyone is home. Spend time talking about your days. You can even have a little snack together as you connect.

Another way you could connect is to take time to pray for one another before everyone heads to bed. Even ten or fifteen minutes together is better than not connecting at all.

The way we initiate family dinners affects the outcome. Remember to present it as something you get to do as a family instead of something you have to do, so your kids will want to take part in family dinners. Mark it on the calendar so your kids know that hour is not free. If a friend invites them over at a scheduled time, be diligent about finding another time your child can visit them. That way, you communicate the priority of your family dinner plus the importance of connecting with friends.

Dinner Discussions

Jonathan and I want to be more intentional in going deeper with the questions we ask our kids at the dinner table. Now that they're older, they'll give more complex answers. We decided to get more creative with our questions. You can use our list below with your family. Remember to answer the questions yourself too. Kids love getting to know their parents better.

1. What's the first thing you would do if you were president?
2. What do you worry about most?

3. What would you change about your school?
4. Which animal would you love to be for a day?
5. What is the hardest thing you've ever done?
6. If you could have any view from your bedroom window, what would it be?

Parents can find countless lists of questions on Pinterest. Type "Questions to ask your kids" in the search bar. From there, you can create a document with the questions. Next, print them out and cut them into strips of paper. Store them in a jar or bucket to use at dinnertime.

When you start this question time, you may experience resistance. Your teenagers may even roll their eyes. I encourage you to push through the resistance, because they secretly enjoy this time. You can also mix things up by putting one child in charge of pulling the question out of the jar. Enjoy this time of getting to know your children.

Silly Day

How many times have you asked your kids to get their elbows off the table, sit on their bottoms, or pull in their chairs? Probably too many times. It gets old, doesn't it? My husband and I decided to do something about this. And that is how Silly Day was born in the Corbin household.

On Silly Day, our kids can sit on their knees, sideways, or whatever way works. Elbows are allowed on the table. The kids can eat with their hands and talk with their mouths full. They are even allowed to burp out loud. Our kids love Silly Day! And to be totally honest, I love it also because I get to say yes to my kids. I enjoy letting them have a rule-free dinner. I dare you to try Silly Day. I am sure your kids will love it, and you might even like it too.

Ways to Come Together

In this chapter we looked at several ways to come together as a family. Family fun night helps children to feel they have a place to belong. It also helps family members learn to laugh together and enjoy each other's company. Family devotions connect your family to our ultimate source of wisdom: God. As we teach our kids to dig into God's Word, they learn that he will always be with them.

Family vacations are a great way to build family identity. As you experience new places, you get to know one another in different settings. Family dinners can build a stronger family bond. These dinners communicate to our children that they are worth our time.

Which one of these items would you like to add to your Intentional Backpack? What step you can make today to add it?

———◦◦◦———

> Let us think of ways to motivate one another to acts of love and good works. And let us not neglect our meeting together, as some people do, but encourage one another, especially now that the day of his return is drawing near. (Hebrews 10:24–25)

This verse teaches us the importance of motivating one another to love others well and do things for others. Parents can model this by loving our family members and others well. As we learn to love each other within our family, we can better love others.

God did not intend us to do life alone. Instead, He provides fellow believers to encourage us and wants us to do the same with other believers. This is why it's important to be involved in a church body. As we meet each Sunday and possibly Wednesdays at our churches, we show our kids the importance of meeting together and encouraging others in their walks with the Lord.

Pack Your Backpack: Choose One Action Step
1. Which of the family fun ideas from this chapter (or an idea of your own) could you do in the next two weeks? Mark a date and time in your calendar.
2. How do you need to prepare for family fun night? (For example, pick up ice cream, make popcorn, reserve a location.)
3. Plan a vacation destination brainstorming session with your family. Pick one idea presented in the chapter to help you begin saving now for a family vacation.
4. Decide how many days a week you would like to have family dinners. Pick the days and add them to your calendar.
5. Write down five questions you could answer at your family dinner and use them.

6. Find a devotional and/or Bible that would work well for your family. Start with one day a week for family devotions. Add another day the following week. Keep building from there.

———◆———

Let us think of ways to motivate one another to acts of love and good works. And let us not neglect our meeting together, as some people do, but encourage one another, especially now that the day of his return is drawing near. (Hebrews 10:24–25)

Please read Hebrews 10:24–25 again. Before reading, ask the Holy Spirit to reveal something new to you. After reading, please answer the study questions below.

1. What is one way you can show love to others?

_____
_____
_____
_____

2. Have you ever neglected meeting with other believers? If so, how did it affect you? If not, why do you keep meeting with other believers?

_____
_____
_____
_____

3. Name five ways you can encourage someone.

_____
_____
_____

4. Pick one of those ways from your list and note it below.

_____
_____
_____

5. Pull out your calendar and mark down when you will encourage someone, then follow through.

Gentle Challenge
This chapter was packed with ideas for gathering with your family. Choose one and use it next week. After doing the activity, reflect on how each family member reacted.

Encouragement
It takes time to form new patterns. Your children, especially teens, might resist at first. Push through the resistance. Enjoy spending time together, knowing you are creating a place for your children to belong.

Let's Pray
Dear God, thank you for our precious family. We take part in so many activities that our calendars quickly fill up. Please help us to make time in our calendar to gather our family. Please guide us to use our time well, especially as we read and study your Word together. Thank you, Holy Spirit, for your help. In Jesus' name, amen.

Please write your own prayer here:
_____
_____
_____
_____

Journal
_____
_____
_____
_____
_____
_____
_____

CHAPTER 2
Celebrate the Good Times

———◆———

Celebrate this Festival of Unleavened Bread, for it will remind you that I brought your forces out of the land of Egypt on this very day. This festival will be a permanent law for you; celebrate this day from generation to generation.

Exodus 12:17

My friend Sarah did not get to enjoy her thirteenth birthday party. Can you even imagine? A week or so prior to the party, she got in trouble and was grounded from everything. Her birthday party at the Family Fun Center had already been paid for, so instead of canceling, her parents made her sit at the table all afternoon while her friends enjoyed the fun. Sarah's parents communicated to her that spending lots of money to impress other parents was more important than their daughter. My heart aches for my friend.

Sarah sat there at her birthday party longing to join in the games. She felt both pain and anger as she watched her friends taking lap after lap on the go-karts and bumper boats. She didn't understand why her friends got to enjoy this party but she couldn't.

Birthdays are special. They are days set aside each year to celebrate your life. I don't know what your experiences were with childhood birthday parties, but maybe you can identify with my friend's experience. Birthday parties should be filled with joy and fun.

Celebrations bring families together and help make lasting memories. As the family gathers and creates traditions, members find comfort and security because they have a place to belong. Family traditions are often passed from generation to generation so children can get to know their heritage. When they understand their past and know they belong to something bigger than themselves, they feel more confident.

There are countless ways to honor one another. In this chapter we will look at a few of those ways. Celebrating as a family bonds you in a special way. As your children move out and start families of their own, they will remember all the ways the family celebrated.

Birthdays

I absolutely love birthdays! When I was a child, my mom cooked my favorite meal, I didn't have to do any chores, and we had a party. It was the one day each year that I looked forward to because I felt loved and important.

Each of us is fearfully and wonderfully made by God (Psalm 139:14). Birthdays are days to celebrate your children's uniqueness and to focus on building up your children and reminding them how wonderful they are.

Our children's birthday parties with friends are generally a different day. The kids pick out a meal for the party and their favorite cake and ice cream. They are allowed to invite five friends and plan the activities they want to do.

The summer our son Nathan turned ten, he wanted to have a water gun fight with his friends. It was a blast for all involved (no pun intended). When our daughter Micaela turned twelve, we invited a few classmates to a party at our friend's pool. Micaela loved hanging out with her friends.

Birthdays are a day to focus on the individual child. It reminds them how special they are. These celebrations help the child to know they belong to a tribe—a group of people that values the child's life.

We love to use birthdays as a time to share affirmations. Each family member shares three things they appreciate about the birthday person. It's a precious time to hear from everyone. It pours confidence into the child and teaches other family members to value who God created the person to be.

Our son Caleb loves to check the mail. One year he kept looking for mail addressed to him and always came back from the mailbox disappointed. It was close to his birthday at that time, so I posted a message on Facebook, asking my friends to mail birthday cards to Caleb. He was over-the-top excited to receive so many cards in the mail.

Another fun birthday tradition is to wake the birthday child in a special way. The family could sing "Happy Birthday." You could also start the decorating the night before. Wrap your child's door in birthday wrapping paper. Add streamers and balloons around the house and include a birthday sign. When they get up in the morning, they will be greeted with decorations. If your older child goes to bed around the same time as you or later, set an alarm to get up early to decorate the house.

We also have a special birthday plate and glass that we set at our child's place at the table the night before. They use these special dishes all day long. Our children choose their favorite breakfast, and we prepare that for them. We also cook their favorite dinner meal. It's fun to see what their current favorite meals are. Another birthday perk is that they have the day off from chores.

Our friends Jeremiah and Marcie have a sweet birthday tradition. They serve breakfast in bed to the birthday person. Their kids love this tradition, as do the parents. Each child has favorite breakfast foods and looks forward to eating their birthday breakfast in bed.

Answered Prayers

One of my favorite ways to celebrate is calling attention to God's faithfulness in answering prayers. When we were first married, Jonathan and I started keeping a record of answered prayers and God's provision. I love this notebook because it is a testimony to our awesome God.

We don't write in our notebook as faithfully as we used to, but we still celebrate answered prayers. This happens either individually with one of our children or sometimes as a family.

I love calling attention to God's faithfulness with even the simplest of prayers. Sometimes my kids will remind me to praise after an answered prayer. I love this because they are watching and seeing God working in their lives.

How did our kids get to this point? Mostly because Jonathan and I have modeled it in our own lives before our kids could talk. Every time God answered a prayer or moved in our lives, we praised Him out loud for the specific answer God gave. As soon as our kids started talking, they always repeated, "Praise the Lord," just like Mommy and Daddy.

You can also start an "Answered Prayers" notebook. Use it to keep track of your answered prayers. After writing in your notebook, have a dance party or listen to a praise song to worship God together.

Another option to celebrate answered prayers is with a blessing basket. Use an index card or slip of paper to document your answered prayer. Place these cards or papers in a basket or jar. Once or twice a year, pull out this jar and read each praise. Celebrate all God has done! You can also read the papers in the jar when you feel down or discouraged. It's a helpful way to set your mind on God and remember all He has pulled you through.

Half Birthdays

Another way to celebrate and pour into your kids, making them feel valuable and loved, is by celebrating half birthdays. For example, our daughter Analiah's birthday is October 13, so her half birthday is April 13.

On our children's half birthdays, they get to use the birthday plate and cup all day long. In the morning, they find a half dollar and half of a birthday card at their place at the table. Later in the day, the birthday child will receive a snack: half of a cupcake from a local bakery.

Our oldest daughter's birthday is June 25, so that means her half birthday is on Christmas Day. To separate the holidays and spread out the celebration, we celebrate her half birthday the day after Christmas.

Salvation Birthdays

Our friends Joel and Lael celebrate their children's salvation birthdays. I love this idea because it focuses on the day the children were born again in Jesus.

On the day that each of their kids made Jesus their forever Friend, Joel and Lael documented that day with a picture so they could keep track of it. The kids' salvation birthday is similar to other birthdays. Joel and Lael give their children a card and buy a gift that will help them grow in their spiritual walk with Jesus. Sometimes the gift is a devotional book or a new Bible. One year they brought their older kids a dry-erase board to write Scripture memory verses on.

I want to be more intentional with celebrating our kids' salvation birthdays. This celebration reminds children that they are involved in something much bigger than themselves. Their worth and value lie in Jesus alone, and when they celebrate this day, they are reminded once again that they belong to Jesus.

Welcome to Womanhood Party

Another celebration to add to your Intentional Backpack is a Welcome to Womanhood party. You can have this party when your daughter starts her monthly period. All too often, the monthly period is considered an unpleasant experience. This party is a way to celebrate the beauty of becoming a woman.

I did not tell our guests that Micaela had started her period. This is not information they needed to know. It was just a marker for me to know when to celebrate Micaela's Welcome to Womanhood party. Rather than having the party after your daughter starts her first period, you could have it for your daughter when she turns thirteen years old.

The first step in planning this party is making a list of several influential women in your daughter's life. Send an invitation with instructions about the night, using the example below as a guide.

Please join us in celebrating _____'s journey into womanhood. We would like you to be part of this night because you have played a special role in _____'s life, and we are grateful.

Please bring a note of encouragement for _____ as she journeys into womanhood. It could be an important truth that has helped you or a Scripture verse that has been meaningful to you and/or reminds you who you are in Christ. Please let _____ know how it has helped you in your journey of becoming the woman God wants you to be. We will present these notes to _____ at the party.

Gifts are not expected, but please feel free to bring one that will encourage her in the womanhood journey.

Thank you so much for being a part of this special night to celebrate _____!

Finger foods and desserts will be served.

Micaela helped me plan the food for the evening. She also gave me a list of people she wanted to invite, and we talked about the influential women in her life.

We decorated the house and started with food and fellowship. Next came a special time. Each woman read Micaela her letter of encouragement about womanhood. If the woman brought a gift, she explained its significance. Many tears and love surrounded Micaela that night.

Afterward, I gathered all the letters and placed them in a scrapbook for Micaela. This is one night we will never forget.

Welcome to Manhood Camping Trip

After our son Nathan turned thirteen, we celebrated the transition to his teenage years with a Welcome to Manhood camping trip. You can add this celebration to your Intentional Backpack.

Jonathan took Nathan to a campground in Michigan, where they fished and hiked. They talked about what it means to be a man. I am thankful for Jonathan pouring into Nathan in this way.

Another option for this Welcome to Manhood camping trip is letting your son invite some of his friends and their fathers to the event. It would be a great way to connect with other men and their boys.

If you're a single mom, I encourage you to ask your father or brother to take your son on this trip. Or you can ask a trusted male friend from your small group at church. It is important for your son to have a man pouring into him, especially at this time.

Holidays

Holidays are another way to celebrate with your family. Once again, your traditions give children a sense of identity and belonging. And when they have their own families, they will be intentional about implementing these traditions.

Jonathan and I come from very different backgrounds. Most couples do. Instead of observing my family traditions or Jonathan's family traditions, we decided to make our own.

Each couple needs to discuss what childhood traditions they like and don't like. Then they can create their own. This can be challenging. But it is healthy and beneficial for the whole family because it gives children a sense of identity, strengthens the family bond, and connects generations by keeping cultural traditions alive.

Once you have decided on traditions, begin celebrating. Kids love being a part of it all. Here are several of our own traditions, by holiday, in addition to many other ideas. I wanted to give you several ideas to spark your own ideas.

New Year's Eve

We make special snacks of smokies wrapped in crescent rolls and veggies with dip. We also toast with sparkling grape juice in wine glasses. Then we gather in the living room and watch a slide show of the pictures from the previous year. Each month throughout the year, I choose forty pictures that best represent what we did that month. It's fun to remember all our events and activities.

Alternately, you could invite another family to join you. Encourage them to bring their pictures from the year too. This would be a fun way to connect.

Sometimes we celebrate New Year's Eve by dressing up in fancy clothes. Help the kids pick out fun outfits, and don't forget to dress fancy too. Have fun with your outfits.

Head to a dollar store or party store to get New Year's Eve supplies. Get a few packs of balloons and blow them up, and get some helium balloons too. Buy some fun hats and party glasses with the new year on them. Don't forget the silly string, streamers, and noisemakers.

Turn the evening into a game night. Try some interactive games such as Twister or Pictionary. You could also have a scavenger hunt with a prize at the end.

Invite another family over for New Year's Eve. Ask them to bring some fun foods and enjoy being together. Do any activities or games with the family mentioned above.

If you can stay up late enough, watch the countdown on TV. Or create your own countdown to celebrate the new year. The day before, prepare balloons for each hour until midnight. At the hour, pop these balloons for the countdown. To add a little more fun, write down an activity to do at that hour and add it to the balloon before you fill it up.

You could adapt the hourly balloon idea by filling bags with activities instead. Each bag needs to be labeled with the hour. At the hour, have your children open the bag and enjoy the activity.

One more idea for New Year's Eve is to conduct a video interview about the previous year with each family member. Start by having your child tell their name, age, and the year.

Ask them questions such as:

1. What was your favorite memory from last year?
2. What new activity do you hope to do next year?
3. What is your favorite food?
4. What is your favorite toy or game from this past year?
5. What is your favorite movie from this year?

New Year's Day
Our family goes out to dinner at a sit-down restaurant every New Year's Day. It's a special treat because we don't do this often. This way, when we do go out, it feels special.

At the dinner, we usually talk about what we enjoyed most from the previous year. We also talk about the things we didn't enjoy. It helps our children to voice disappointments in a safe environment. We end the evening by talking about what we look forward to most in the new year.

Begin your New Year's Day with a breakfast. But not just any breakfast. Make pancakes and then cut out the numbers of the year. Another breakfast idea is a yummy breakfast casserole or just scrambled eggs and bacon. Choose the foods your family enjoys.

Head to your library before New Year's Day and find books about this holiday. Read them to learn the history of New Year's Day. There are also several New Year's Day children's books to read with your kids.

Here are a few book titles to look for:

- *P. Bear's New Year's Party: A Counting Book* by Paul Owen Lewis
- *Squirrel's New Year's Resolution* by Pat Miller
- *Happy New Year Everywhere!* by Arlene Erlbach
- *The Night Before New Year's* by Natasha Wing
- *Freedom Soup* by Tami Charles
- *Shanté Keys and the New Year's Peas* by Gail Piernas-Davenport
- *The Stars Will Still Shine* by Cynthia Rylant
- *Every Month Is a New Year: Celebrations Around the World* by Marilyn Singer
- *Happy New Year, Spot!* by Eric Hill
- *New Year's Day* by Mari C. Schuh

Another idea for New Year's Day is writing a family letter. In the letter, write about the major events of the past year. Also include what you look forward to in the coming year. Keep these letters in a file or jar. Each year, as you write a new letter, take time to read over the letters from the years before. The file or jar in which you store the letters can be a time capsule of sorts.

Have a New Year's Day campout! Set up your tent in the living room. If you don't have a tent, create a fort with blankets and chairs. Get creative and make a "fire" out of orange and yellow construction paper for your campout. Be sure to have hot cocoa and fun snacks too.

Start an "Out with the Old" tradition. Have your kids go through their bedrooms for any books, toys, games, and stuffed animals they no longer use. Parents can do this too. Put it all in boxes and take it to a thrift store to bless someone else. Another "Out with the Old" option is rearranging your furniture in your living room and/or bedrooms. That way, you have something fresh and new for the year. Get everyone involved and have fun!

Another idea is to have a craft time together. Gather craft materials from a dollar store and get creative. Have the kids make whatever they want, or look up New Year's Day-specific crafts on Pinterest.

One more idea for New Year's Day is a movie marathon. Pick a movie series or several different movies to watch. Make popcorn, grab some other snacks, and enjoy snuggling together on the couch while watching the movies.

Valentine's Day

The night before Valentine's Day, Jonathan and I cut out one big heart and three small hearts for each child. On the big heart, we write the child's name. On the smaller hearts, we write a character trait we appreciate about that child.

In the morning, the hearts are on taped on their bedroom doors. Our kids love this because it speaks into who they are and affirms them as people. Jonathan and I love pouring truth into their hearts.

We also get our kids small gifts and candy. I enjoy making a heart-themed breakfast, like heart-shaped pancakes or eggs in a nest. Making this breakfast takes time, but it communicates to my children that they are worth my time and that I value bringing them joy.

One year we sent our kids Valentine's Day cards in the mail. We picked up the cards from a dollar store and wrote a note to each child. The kids loved this because they got real mail. And they appreciated the notes.

Another fun tradition is to send Valentine's Day cards to the grandparents, other family members, and friends. Plan a time to sit down together as a family and write notes in the cards. You can even make your own homemade cards to send. The family members and friends will love receiving mail. Another idea is to make cards for widows in your church. It would be a great way encourage them and remind them they are loved and seen.

Plan a fancy dinner for your family. Include red, white, and/or pink foods in your menu. Get creative with the food. Decorate the table with hearts and candles to create a fun atmosphere. Pick up Valentine's Day plates and napkins from a dollar store. Plan a special dessert for the kids—one you don't make often. Serve sparkling grape juice in wine glasses. If you don't have wine glasses, consider getting some for these special occasions. Dollar stores have some nice ones.

Another way to celebrate Valentine's Day is to make Valentine's Day cards with Scripture verses on them, such as John 3:16, which talks about the ultimate love. You could also use 1 John 4:19.

> For God so loved the world that He gave His one and only Son, that whoever believes in Him shall not perish but have eternal life. (John 3:16)

> We love each other because He loved us first. (1 John 4:19)

On each card, write "God Loves You." You can also include your church information to help people get plugged into a church. Take these cards to nearby parks and pass them out. If the weather is not favorable, give them to people in your neighborhood or another neighborhood you are familiar with.

Around Valentine's Day, you can usually find gummy candies in X and O shapes. Use these gummies to play tic-tac-toe. Create and laminate your own board or find one on the internet. The winner of the game gets to eat the gummies. You may want to play this game early in the day.

One year, Papa John's sold heart-shaped pizzas on Valentine's Day. That was a fun way to celebrate. The kids love pizza, so it was a win. If heart-shaped pizza isn't available, make your own. Pick up some premade crusts (or use homemade) and cut the dough into a heart shape. Add your sauce, toppings, and cheese. Enjoy eating your heart-shaped pizza!

Who said Valentine mailboxes are only for the classroom? About two weeks before Valentine's Day, create some mailboxes together and have each child create their own. If your child is younger, assist as needed. We have many options for creating mailboxes, including shoeboxes or tissue boxes. Decorate the outside with hearts and Valentine's Day colors. Use construction paper and stickers. Have fun decorating it. Make sure to label it with your name.

Another option is to head to a craft or department store and pick up cute mailboxes. Decorate them with stickers of all sorts, including letter stickers for your names. You can be as simple or creative as you desire with these mailboxes.

On the first of February, set them out. Encourage your family members to write love notes to one another throughout the days leading up to Valentine's Day. It's a great way to pour encouragement into each other.

Another fun thing we have done is a Valentine treasure hunt. Hide clues, written on heart-shaped paper, around the house. Make as many clues as you desire, depending on your kids' ages. At the end of the hunt, let them find a large box of candy or another fun surprise.

Consider creating a "What I Love about You" scrapbook to write in each year. Family members take turns writing down one thing they love the most about each other. As the years go on, you can continue to look back at this and remember all the fun times you have had together.

Valentine's coupons are another great tradition to start with your family. Include coupons for late bedtime, soda at dinner, outing with Mom, outing with Dad, extra dessert, ten minutes of extra snuggles at bedtime, thirty minutes of extra screen time, ice cream, and a family movie and pizza night. Give these coupon books to your kids on Valentine's Day. They can use them throughout the year.

Easter

My mom's side of the family has a Slovak heritage. My favorite part of Easter was all the yummy ethnic food we made. First, we made ponina, which is pork and veal mixed with fresh parsley, garlic, and eggs. Pressed together like meatloaf, it cooks in a glass pan. We also made homemade cheese called hrutka and a bread called paska.

To teach the kids my heritage, Jonathan and I decided to make this a part of our Easter traditions. Over the years we've adjusted the recipes due to my food allergies, but we still have a version of this special food. I love sharing these foods with our kids so they can develop a connection with their ancestors.

I love our Easter traditions of putting Easter baskets at the table for our kids. We fill them with candy and a small toy. My friend Tara fills her kids' Easter baskets with devotionals or books that help her children grow closer to Jesus.

We love to invite our neighbors to our Easter service, as our pastor always gives a salvation message. Our church hosts an Easter egg hunt for the community. Before the big day, they hand out empty plastic eggs for church members to fill with candy. Our family loves to fill those together.

On Easter, we sometimes help set up the Easter egg hunt. It's a great way to serve our community together. If your church doesn't have an Easter egg hunt, consider hosting a small one at your home for neighborhood kids. This is a great way to minister to others and tell them about our hope in Jesus.

We also love to have an egg hunt at home for our kids. In the past, we've filled the eggs with candy. Lately, we have started to fill the eggs differently. We cut slips of paper and write "Fifteen minutes of individual time with Mom," "Fifteen minutes of individual time with Dad," "One day with no chores," or "Thirty minutes of screen time." The kids love these options. We also have an alleluia egg. It's a larger egg filled with money. Jonathan usually hides this egg in a hard-to-find place. It's a big deal to find this egg.

On Easter, a friend from our old church always opened their home to single people or church members without family in the area. They also invited neighbors. I love how they ministered to people. It was also a great opportunity to share Jesus with those who didn't know the real reason we celebrate Easter.

Another fun Easter tradition is to egg your neighbors. I promise, they will enjoy it. Fill an Easter basket with goodies—maybe some baked goods, candy-filled eggs, or a small gift. Include a Scripture verse card about Jesus. Get creative and have fun. Don't forget to include a card that says "You've been egged with love" and signed with your family name.

When I was a little girl, we often got a new dress for Easter and sometimes an Easter hat. This was a big deal for us five girls. I felt beautiful in my new dress, and my brothers always looked handsome in their new dress clothes. Consider doing this tradition to celebrate Jesus's resurrection.

Another idea is making jelly bean bags to hand out to the kids in your neighborhood or share with your kids' friends. Fill the bag with all sorts of jelly bean colors. Here is a list of the colors and what they stand for. Write or type up this information to include on the outside of the bags.

Black is for our sin, the ways we break God's rules.
Red is for the blood of Jesus, shed on the cross so we may have eternal life.
White is for purity, which we receive when we believe in Jesus.
Orange is for the Holy Spirit, who lives in us when we receive Jesus.
Green is for growth, reading the Bible, and learning about Jesus.
Gold is for the streets of heaven, which we will see someday.
Purple is for royalty. You are a child of the King of Kings.
Pink is for God's love.

Sometimes, our family makes resurrection rolls on Easter. You'll need large marshmallows, a package of crescent rolls, cinnamon and sugar mixed in a bowl, and a little water. Gather everyone at the table with the ingredients laid out. Preheat the oven to 350 degrees.

Read John 19 together, then unroll the crescent rolls and separate each section. Explain to your children that this is like the cloth they wrapped Jesus in. Next, hand each person a marshmallow. Explain that the pure, white marshmallow represents Jesus because He is without sin.

The next step is to dip the marshmallow in a small bowl of water. This symbolizes the embalming oils mentioned in John 19:39. Roll the marshmallow in the cinnamon and sugar mixture. This represents the spices used to prepare Jesus' body for burial (John 19:40).

Next, wrap the marshmallow in the crescent roll dough and pinch the sides closed. This represents how they wrapped Jesus' body. Repeat this process for all the marshmallows. Place the rolls in the oven, which symbolizes the tomb. Bake according to the time specified on the package.

While the rolls bake, read John 20:1–18 together. Once the rolls are done, open the "tomb" and remove the rolls. Once they are cooled, let your children open a roll to see what happened to the marshmallow. They will see that it has disappeared. This signifies that Jesus has resurrected from the dead. Enjoy eating this fun treat together.

Another tradition we follow is coloring Easter eggs. I boil the eggs ahead of time so we are ready to go. Also, make sure to save some newspapers to spread out on the table to protect it. Jonathan figured out that coloring the boiled eggs while they are still slightly warm makes the colors pop, and they are easier to handle than cold eggs.

We line up coffee cups filled with egg dye. The kids each get the same number of eggs to color. Even Jonathan and I color eggs. It's a fun tradition.

When I was a kid, one of my favorite Easter traditions was cracking the eggs on my sibling's heads. My seven siblings and I had a little too much fun with it. We have done this with our kids, and they love it. You definitely need to put parameters in place to make sure eggs aren't slammed too hard on the head. That may or may not have happened when I was a kid.

Independence Day

Our kids love sparklers, so that has become one of our traditions for July Fourth. One year, the older kids each picked out a new firework. Nathan chose smoke bombs, and Micaela wanted large neon sparklers. I enjoyed watching them decide which to get. When we set off those fireworks, the pure joy in their eyes was fun to see. Analiah and Caleb yelled that the new fireworks were cool, and Jonathan and I agreed. The pride flashing in Micaela and Nathan's eyes was precious because they heard from us that they have great ideas.

On July 4, we also celebrate with yummy snacks and food. Our son Nathan looks forward to this holiday (his love language is food). One year he gave twenty dollars of his birthday money toward the July Fourth food. It ended up being mostly desserts and junk food, but that was okay. Why? Because we let the kids pick, and by doing that, we celebrated who they were.

This past July Fourth, our son Nathan bought a huge box of fireworks. We also picked up smoke bombs, Pop-Its, and sparklers. We invited a family to come over to hang out and see the fireworks. They brought some snacks, and we had several set out too.

It was great watching Nathan light all the fireworks from the box. (Jonathan was right there to assist and keep things safe.) The fireworks show was amazing! It was so much fun to be home and see fireworks. Several people in our neighborhood also set off fireworks. We enjoyed watching them all as the night went on.

Another fun tradition is picking a special spot for the family to go every year. It could be a nearby park for a picnic lunch. Or maybe it's a trip to the beach, a hike at a nearby state park, or going out for ice cream. This tradition is flexible. Once you have decided on a place, make sure to go there every year on the Fourth of July. Your family will look forward to it each year.

The Fourth of July is a great time to have a cookout, so fire up the grill. Cook your family favorites, such as brats, hot dogs, and hamburgers. Don't forget the watermelon and corn on the cob. Invite your neighbors and/or other families to join you. Pick up some patriotic decorations at a dollar store. Put one of your kids in charge of decorations. Have fun being festive.

Another way to celebrate is with food traditions. When I was younger, my grandma always made a Fourth of July cake. It had whipped cream as the main layer, with blueberries and strawberries on top, shaped like an American flag. As a child, I always looked forward to seeing the cake. I didn't want to ruin it by cutting it, since it was so pretty. But we did anyway.

You can also make a patriotic breakfast of pancakes with whipped cream, blueberries, and strawberries. The kids will love it. We also like July Fourth ice cubes. Pick up bottles of red, white, and blue sports drinks. Fill ice cube trays with each color. Freeze them and enjoy them in water or sparkling water.

Each July Fourth, take a patriotic family photo. Get your family dressed up in red, white, and blue. A dollar store may even have some fun patriotic items to use in your picture. If you're hosting a cookout that day, set up a photo booth where other families can get their picture taken too.

Another fun Fourth of July tradition is hosting a bike parade. Invite the neighborhood kids to join. Decorate the bikes with streamers and any other July Fourth decorations you have. Ride around your neighborhood, showing off your American spirit.

Thanksgiving

One of our favorite Thanksgiving traditions is watching the Macy's Thanksgiving Day parade together. This tradition is more recent than others, since our kids are older now and can appreciate the parade more. It's fun to snuggle on the couch together and exclaim over the floats. I love telling the kids how I used to watch the parade when I was their age. So much about the parade has changed over the years, so it's fun to talk about that with our kids. It is very special to now share this tradition with them. It reminds our kids they are part of something bigger.

The Saturday after Thanksgiving has become our Christmas decorating day. We used to enjoy picking out a real tree together. Narrowing our choices to one tree was an adventure. Jonathan and I let the kids give their opinions on which tree to get.

Afterward, we head home, set up the tree, and begin decorating. After the lights are on, Jonathan hangs special ornaments on the tree before all the others. Once he says go, the kids cover the tree with ornaments of all kinds.

The past several Christmases, we have used an artificial tree. A couple of years ago, our older kids went to the shed and pulled out the tree, then they set it up on their own. I love how they took initiative and ownership of the tree.

If you prefer a real tree, make a tradition out of picking one up. Find a tree farm, even if you have to travel a distance. Each year, make the trip to the same tree farm to pick out your tree. My sister Clare keeps this tradition. When all the siblings and our families come to her home after Thanksgiving, we caravan to the tree farm. It's fun to be there when she picks out her tree. After this past year, Jonathan and I are considering making this our tradition too. There is something special about picking a specific tree and cutting it down.

Another way to celebrate Thanksgiving with your family is to create personalized name cards. Use a half sheet on cardstock folded in half, and write one family member or guest's name on each sheet. When the meal is over, pass around the cards. Have each person write one thing they love or appreciate about the person named on their card. Each person will leave with a card full of encouragement to look at throughout the year.

Another Thanksgiving tradition idea is moving your feet. Find a Turkey Trot and run or walk it with your family and/or friends. If a Turkey Trot isn't available in your area, create your own. Map out a 5K route and invite your neighbors and/or friends to join in the fun. Another option is to take a walk soon after your Thanksgiving meal. Walk around the block. Take your time and enjoy being together. A big bonus is walking off all those calories and making room for dessert.

Host a Friendsgiving at your house for your closest friends and their families on a day close to Thanksgiving. Ask everyone to bring a side dish or dessert while you provide the turkey or other main dish. Play games or craft together. Enjoy spending time with one another.

Cover your Thanksgiving table with butcher paper. Lay out different colored markers or plain black ones. Invite your family and any guests to write down things they are thankful for from the past year. Another option is to cover a card table with the butcher paper and ask each person to write down what they are grateful for. That way your butcher paper doesn't get covered with Thanksgiving food. Be sure to date the paper and look back at it over the years to come.

Another fun Thanksgiving tradition is to have a space stocked with Thanksgiving coloring sheets, crayons, and markers. That way the kids can color while waiting for the meal to start. At this same space, have some easy Thanksgiving crafts prepared for the kids. You could also get them involved in making the place cards if they are old enough. Let them be creative and do it how they want. Or look up place card ideas and provide materials and instructions.

Thanksgiving usually involves football. Even if you are not a football fan, it's fun to relax on the couch and watch a game. Another option is to play a game of touch football with family and friends before or after dinner.

It's a great way to be active together and have fun too. Maybe the winners get dessert first. It's always more fun to play for a prize.

One more Thanksgiving tradition is writing thank-you notes. Have your family members and/or guests think of someone who made a difference in their lives this past year. Then hand them a thank-you card to write to this person. After the cards are done, address envelopes and send them out the next day.

Christmas Eve

Each year, we alternate between giving our kids new pajamas or slippers for Christmas. This is the one gift our kids are allowed to open on Christmas Eve. If it is a pajamas year, I always wash them ahead of time so the kids can wear them that evening.

If your kids are with their other parent on Christmas Eve, and you want to do this tradition, you may need to give the pajamas to them a day earlier. Or you can ask your child's other parent to give the pajamas or slippers to them.

We also love to attend a Christmas Eve service. It's special to worship together as a family and thank God for Jesus' birth. I love being with our church family too. It reminds our children that our family is not just within our walls.

One way to serve on Christmas Eve is to volunteer to help in the church nursery. Our church holds seven Christmas Eve services. This past year, we served in the nursery as a family. It was a special time to love others' children so the parents could enjoy the service. If this isn't an option at your church, volunteer as a family at a soup kitchen in the area. Or shop together for canned goods to donate to a local food bank. Our children's schools always host a food drive for families in the community. It's a great way to give.

Another fun way to celebrate Christmas Eve is to have an ugly Christmas sweater contest. You could invite friends or family to get involved. The uglier the sweater, the better. Have a vote for the ugliest sweater and give a prize to the winner. Be sure to take a picture of all involved to look back on over the years.

Consider making Christmas Eve an all-day pajama day with crafts, games, and baking. Prep simple or complex crafts (depending on the ages of your kids) ahead of time so they are ready to make. Enjoy crafting together. Set up a puzzle table and spend blocks of time working the puzzle throughout the day. Pick a favorite cookie recipe and make it together. Have each family member pick a favorite game. Play each game for ten or fifteen minutes or longer if desired. Spend this day doing all or just a few of these activities.

Find a live nativity in your area. You may not be able to do this on Christmas Eve because of the schedule, but this is a great activity any time during the Christmas season. It's special to see a live depiction of Jesus' birth. It gives a picture of what it was like for Joseph and Mary on that special evening.

Gather your family, friends, and their families and go Christmas caroling. Walk around each other's neighborhoods, spreading Christmas cheer. Afterward, warm up with hot chocolate. Or end the time with pizza and pop. Another option is to record yourselves singing and send the video to other family or friends.

Consider ordering out for your Christmas Eve dinner. Since your Christmas dinner is less than twenty-four hours away, take a break from cooking and order takeout from your favorite restaurant. Use disposable plates, napkins, and forks. The kids can serve themselves. Cleanup will be easy, so you'll have more time to enjoy one another.

Gather to watch a Christmas movie before you go to bed. A few of our favorites are *The Nativity*, *Elf*, *Miracle on 34th Street*, *The Star*, *A Christmas Carol* (our favorite version is the one with George C. Scott as Scrooge), *How the Grinch Stole Christmas,* and the *Home Alone* movies. Make some popcorn and enjoy being together.

One other fun Christmas Eve tradition I have read about is Christmas Eve boxes. We haven't started this tradition yet, but it sounds like fun. The Christmas Eve box is a designated box filled with items that go along with the other traditions mentioned above. In the Christmas Eve box, you could add the Christmas pajamas, a favorite book, popcorn, hot cocoa mix, and a new mug. You could also add a treat or candy. The box can be filled with anything your kids would enjoy. On Christmas Eve, during the day or in the evening, give your children the Christmas Eve box and watch their eyes light up with delight. This Christmas Eve box is meant to be reused every year for your children.

I also love the tradition of exchanging Christmas ornaments on Christmas Eve. Each family member buys or picks out an ornament that represents their favorite family memory from the year. On Christmas Eve, everyone brings their wrapped ornament. One by one, family members choose an ornament from the pile. They open it, and the family member who picked it out explains the favorite memory from the year.

Another option for the Christmas ornaments is to have the parents buy an ornament for each child every year. Then when the child opens it, the parents can explain why they chose that specific ornament. When your children move out, they will have a box of ornaments representing very special memories to take with them.

Christmas Day

I love Christmas! After our Christmas breakfast, we gather on the couch. Jonathan pulls out his Bible and turns to Luke 2. We all listen as he reads the story of Jesus' birth. This tradition is my favorite because Christmas is all about Jesus.

On Christmas Day, we celebrate Jesus by singing to him and enjoying a birthday cake together. In the past, we have baked a regular cake for Jesus. This past year, I tried a new cake with a lot of symbolism.

The cake had three layers. The chocolate layer represented the darkness of sin. The red layer reminded us that Jesus' blood was shed for the forgiveness of our sins. The green layer represented the new life we have in Jesus and how we can grow in Him. The white frosting was for the purity of Jesus, who covers all our sins. Our sins are washed as white as snow. After we sang "Happy Birthday," we talked through each layer and read Scriptures about them. I loved how this helped us focus on the real reason for Christmas.

As a child, I loved St. Nick's Day. On the evening of December fifth, we set out our shoes. In the morning, we found them filled with treats, such as candy, tangerines, and a small toy.

This holiday originated from Nicholas of Myra. He was a bishop in fourth-century Greece. During his lifetime, Nicholas was known for giving gifts, and he especially loved placing coins in other people's shoes.

Nicholas of Myra was the inspiration for our modern Santa Claus. We talk about Santa Claus in our family, but we don't celebrate him. I love celebrating gift giving, which is Jesus' heart. That is why we celebrate St. Nick's Day.

Each year around Christmas, we set up the tripod to get a family picture in front of the tree. As the years go by, we see how much each family member has grown.

This annual picture became a source of frustration for some of our family. Often, when it was time for the picture, we were all in our pajamas and didn't want to go and change. So we did things differently last year—we took our Christmas picture on Christmas Eve. We dressed up for church that day, so before leaving, we set up the tripod. Now we can stay in our pajamas on Christmas instead of taking time to dress up. It went much smoother, and we enjoyed our picture more.

Plan a special breakfast for Christmas morning. Maybe you could serve an egg casserole or cinnamon rolls. Or you could have scrambled eggs, bacon, and toast. If you have Christmas dishes, pull those out. Or, before Christmas, head to a dollar store and get some. They have some fun patterns.

Pile the family in the van and look at Christmas lights. Some people put a lot of work into their Christmas light display. Enjoy looking at them together. Pack some hot cocoa and blankets as you travel. You can add a Christmas scavenger hunt to your drive. Create a list with things such as a nativity scene or a snowman to find on this hunt.

Each year, purchase a new board game for the family. It's a great way to connect and make time to be together. Some of our favorites include Sorry, Qwirkle, and Sequence.

Every evening in December, have each family member take a slip of red or green paper and write one thing they are grateful for from that day. Make a gratitude chain with these papers, hang it somewhere around the house, and watch it grow.

Lots of people write letters to Santa every year. But the real reason for the season is Jesus. Why not write Jesus a letter of gratitude for all He went through for us? Take some time to talk about this letter with your family and remind them of Jesus's love and sacrifice for them. After writing a small and simple letter of gratitude to Jesus, slip it inside a balloon and fill it with helium. As a family, send the balloon up to heaven.

Do you know of a neighbor or friend who could use some food? Gather all the items they would need for a Christmas dinner and place it in a box. This is what you could put in the boxes:

1. A ham
2. Canned green beans
3. Canned yams
4. A bag of marshmallows
5. Brown sugar
6. Canned corn
7. Canned cranberry sauce
8. Stuffing mix
9. Instant mashed potatoes or a box of scalloped or au gratin potatoes
10. Cornbread mix
11. A carton of eggs
12. Macaroni and cheese
13. Dessert (canned pie filling and a crust or a cake mix)
14. Christmas plates, napkins, and plastic silverware

After putting this in a box, pray over the box as a family. Ask God to encourage the recipients and provide for their every need. Pray for them to experience God in a powerful way this Christmas. Next, deliver the Christmas box anonymously to a family. Ring the doorbell and run away before they see you.

One more fun Christmas tradition is a sibling gift exchange. This works well when your kids are older. Have each child write a Christmas wish list. Take each child shopping so they can pick out gifts for their siblings. Help them decide what they can get with the money they have. You can provide money for your kids to shop for each other. Or you can give your children opportunities to earn money so they can pay for the gifts themselves.

Celebrations bring families together and help create lasting memories. In this chapter we looked at a lot of ways to celebrate. Did it spark some ideas for your family? I wish I could hear all about the traditions you are passing on to your children.

Celebrating helps your children to have a place to belong, and it bonds the family in a special way. As your children move out and start families of their own, they will remember all the ways you celebrated when they were small.

Celebrate this Festival of Unleavened Bread, for it will remind you that I brought your forces out of the land of Egypt on this very day. This festival will be a permanent law for you; celebrate this day from generation to generation. (Exodus 12:17)

Exodus 12 begins with God giving specific instructions to Moses and Aaron, telling them exactly how to celebrate Passover. God wanted His people to remember this special night. He wanted them to celebrate year after year and pass down the customs from generation to generation. God was clear that this holiday would celebrate His faithfulness.

When we celebrate holidays and events with our children, it reminds them that they are part of something bigger. As we celebrate traditions passed down from generation to generation, we connect our children with their heritage. Celebrating also gives us many opportunities to see how God is faithful. We can point them back to the many ways God has come through.

Pack Your Backpack: Choose One Action Step

1. Pick up a notebook and begin documenting answered prayers with your family.

2. Anytime God answers a prayer, celebrate with your family by saying, "Praise the Lord for _____."

3. Choose one new way to celebrate your children's birthdays, using this chapter as a guide. Plan to shop for any items you need before the birthday.
4. Celebrate your child's salvation birthday. If you don't know the exact date, pick a date close to the time your child asked Jesus to be their Savior.
5. Sit down with your spouse and discuss holiday traditions. Do you want to add any new traditions? Talk about the ones you want to get rid of as well.
6. Pick one holiday tradition mentioned in this chapter and use it with your family.

———◦———

> Celebrate this Festival of Unleavened Bread, for it will remind you that I brought your forces out of the land of Egypt on this very day. This festival will be a permanent law for you; celebrate this day from generation to generation. (Exodus 12:17)

Please reread Exodus 12:1–17. Before reading, ask the Holy Spirit to reveal something new to you. After reading, please answer the study questions below.

1. Why did God have the Israelites spread blood on the sides and tops of the doorframes?

_____

_____

_____

_____

2. What specific instructions did God give for the way to eat the meal?

_____

_____

_____

_____

3. Why does God want them to remember this day?

_____

_____

_____

_____

4. List five ways God has delivered you from a hard situation.

_____

_____

_____

_____

5. Why is it important to celebrate?

_____

_____

_____

_____

Gentle Challenge

This chapter was packed with ideas for celebrations. Choose one to incorporate in the next week. After doing the activity, reflect on how each family member reacted.

Encouragement

Social media is full of ways to celebrate. Often, we compare ourselves to other moms. We wonder why we can't seem to do all the fun things. I encourage you to choose activities that work well for the season you're in. If you can do one thing well, you've made a difference for your children. Don't try to do it all. Your presence in your kids' lives is more important than what you do.

Let's Pray

Dear God, thank you for the gift of celebrating. Please help us to celebrate well in our family. Thank you, Holy Spirit, for your wisdom and for showing us ways to celebrate in this season of life. Help us to celebrate your

faithfulness, God, and reflect on it often. May we always point to you in all we say and do. In Jesus' name, amen.

Please write your own prayer here:

_____

_____

_____

_____

Journal

_____

_____

_____

_____

_____

_____

_____

_____

_____

_____

_____

_____

_____

_____

_____

_____

_____

_____

_____

PART TWO

———◆———

Marriage: The Love That Created Your Family Keeps It Together

CHAPTER 3
Your Number One

———◆———

"At last!" the man exclaimed. "This one is bone from my bone,
and flesh from my flesh! She will be called 'woman,' because
she was taken from 'man.'" This explains why a man leaves his
father and mother and is joined to his wife, and the two are
united into one.

Genesis 2:23–24

When I was a girl, I used to think no one else had family problems. I felt alone at times as I wrestled with my parents' constant fighting. One day at school, a friend confided in me that her parents were getting a divorce. She shared how relieved she was, since she didn't have to hear the fighting anymore.

I felt sad for her, mostly because I understood what it felt like to have a home like that. I also felt sorrow for the broken marriage. Even though I didn't personally know God at the time, I did know that marriage was a sacred union and shouldn't be broken.

Family begins at the wedding. The marriage relationship should be our number one priority under God. In Matthew 19:5, we read, "And he said, 'This explains why a man leaves his father and mother and is joined to his wife, and the two are united into one.'" This Scripture verse clearly reminds us that when we marry, we leave our family of origin. All too often, we cling to our family because that's what is comfortable and what we know.

We need to make our marriages the priority relationship, even above our extended family. Of course, you will still be in communication with your family. But when you struggle with something, turn to your spouse instead of calling your mom. When you need help with your car, ask your husband instead of your dad.

The marriage relationship is also above your role as a parent. In the busyness of life, we often forget this truth. Work, including household chores, takes a lot of our time.

When the kids are younger, their needs are demanding. As they get older, their needs change, but the kids still require a lot of time. It's easy to let children become the priority in the family. We must not let this happen, even though it's hard to avoid in our culture.

We must make our marriage relationship our priority. Date nights are one of the best ways to do that.

Date nights can seem daunting. How do we have time in our busy schedules? Honestly, we don't have the time unless we make the time.

Making the Time

Since our marriage is our most important relationship, other than our relationship with God, we should prioritize date nights over all other activities. At the beginning of the week or month, sit down together and schedule a date. Start with one date a month and build from there.

My husband Jonathan and I celebrated twenty-two years of marriage this past June. We have four children, who are all involved in activities. Life is crazy, and I hear it doesn't slow down. That's why we prioritize date nights.

Along with keeping God at the center, weekly date nights help our marriage to thrive. So let's talk a little more about date nights, why we need them, and how to implement them.

A date night is a time to get away with just your spouse. We began weekly dates within the first year of our marriage. Jonathan was a youth pastor at that time and had a lot of meetings. So we decided to guard one night a week for just us. Now, twenty-two years later, we still go on a weekly date.

The purpose of date nights is to connect with your spouse. No matter how long you've been married, there are still things to learn about each other.

It's also wonderful to have adult conversation, especially if you've had a full day with the kids. Sometimes we have more serious talks, and other dates are filled with fun activities. It varies by the week.

People often tell me they can't afford date nights. I generally respond by sharing how we afford it.

First, we have a line in our budget for date nights. It's a priority for us, above kids' activities and sometimes even household items. Our relationship is worth investing in and fighting for.

Second, we don't pay a babysitter. Instead, we swap babysitting with several other families. We watch their kids once a month and vice versa. Our kids love going to their friends' houses, so it's a win-win. Once in a while, we do need to pay a babysitter if plans change with other families. But since we've made that a priority in the budget, it's not a problem.

Date nights are great to add to your Intentional Backpack. They're not only important for your marriage relationship, but they're important for your kids too. Date nights communicate to your children that your marriage is the priority. The other benefit is the security children feel when they see their parents together.

Weekend Getaways

Another way to prioritize your marriage is by taking a weekend getaway at least once a year. If time and the budget allow, try to get away twice a year.

Hocking Hills, Ohio; Ludington, Michigan; Fort Wayne, Indiana; and a hotel across town are just a few of the places we've gone for our anniversary getaways. I believe getaways are vital for the marriage relationship, and here's why:

1. They keep your relationship a priority. After God, your marriage is your number one relationship. This time away at least once a year shows your kids and other family and friends that you value your marriage. It also speaks to your spouse that they are worth your time.

2. They rekindle romance. The demands of work, family life, housework, and yard work are endless. Because of this, it can be hard to keep romance alive. Weekend getaways create a space to rekindle your romance. They give you a chance to focus on you as a couple.
3. They build a stronger relationship. Time spent with another person strengthens the relationship. So when you take time away for your marriage, it will get stronger. A weekend getaway helps you to focus on one another. It gives you uninterrupted time to listen to each other's hopes, dreams, and plans. It also gives you time to dream together.
4. They relax and refresh you both. They force you to leave the demands of home life and jobs behind. Use this time to refuel. Then you'll head back to your regular life refreshed and encouraged. Taking time away helps your other relationships, since you come back renewed.

Implementing Weekend Getaways

Implementing weekend getaways is similar to planning date nights. Make the time for your getaway on your calendar. Sit down together at the beginning of each calendar year and carve out the time before the year begins. Each year, we schedule one of our getaways around our wedding anniversary. It's easy to get on the calendar because we celebrate it every year.

Your weekend getaways are perfect times for your kids to spend time with their grandparents. Ask your parents to spend intentional time with your kids while you're away. Another option is to ask one of your siblings to watch your kids.

We don't have family in the area, so we needed to get creative. In the first church we attended, we got close to a couple and started calling them Mom and Dad. They have five children, so we asked them, "What's two more?" When we first moved to town, Jonathan and I were both in our early twenties, so we felt like kids anyway.

Our kids call Scott and Sarah Grandpa and Grandma. We feel blessed to have "family" we can count on. Our kids absolutely love going to Grandpa and Grandma's during our weekend getaways. In fact, they often don't want to come home.

Other couples need time away too. If you have trusted friends who also have children, consider asking them to swap childcare duties with you. They take your kids during your weekend getaway, and you take theirs when they need a weekend to themselves. Our kids love this option because they get time with their friends.

What Others Are Saying about Weekend Getaways

I asked Jonathan how date nights help our marriage. He said that date nights help by creating space to talk about things that get neglected in the busyness of life. He also believes weekend getaways can create space to have important/deeper conversations that we may not be able to finish in a single sitting.

Next, I asked two of my friends' husbands the same question.

Carl said, "My wife and I enjoy riding in the car together. No music, just chatting. It's a pleasant way to enjoy one another's company—even more than the activity planned for the date. We went to Indianapolis this past weekend. For me, it was refreshing. Spending a few days in a different environment almost makes our home responsibilities vanish as we enjoy one another."

This is James's viewpoint: "My wife feels the weight of almost every responsibility in the home and family, especially when she can physically see it in front of her. We take a two- or three-day anniversary getaway every year. Being away from home helps her to focus on the nonstressful love-connection parts of our relationship. We can talk and plan more clearly. We can laugh and play unguarded, both physically and emotionally. For me, every vacation is all about my wife. If I can get her to destress, relax, and increase her joy, then I consider the whole trip a win. I want to focus on her because her focus is perpetually on everyone and everything else. She deserves the extra appreciation and attention, but it also helps the whole family to bond, grow, and communicate in the next season of life."

Recently, I asked a few friends to tell me what their favorite couple weekend getaway was, and why. It was so fun to read the responses. In fact,

I felt excitement as I thought about all the marriages that were strengthened and kids who were positively affected. Here are some of the responses. Maybe it will help spark an idea or two for your next weekend getaway.

- Amanda: "Nashville. My husband and I are both avid country music lovers."
- Ben: "The Grand Hotel on Mackinaw Island. I have always loved that place due to family adventures as a kid, not to mention *Somewhere in Time*. Anita loved the place as well. I had the best company in the world (my lover). The hotel food was exquisite, and the atmosphere was a true joy."
- Krista: "Las Vegas. It was silly and fairly cheap. We went to comedy shows and just enjoyed laughing together."
- Tonya: "We spent a few days on a tall ship in Lake Michigan. We tried our hand at crewing and also just relaxed. It was an adventure!"
- Janette: "We love St. Joe, Michigan—the beach, the restaurants, and just walking around downtown. Sometimes we drive up for dinner and the sunset if we have only the evening."
- Sabreana: "We love the Rocky Mountains. We went for a long weekend and enjoyed driving through the mountains, as well as Colorado Springs and Garden of the Gods. Such majesty displayed."

Weekend getaways are another thing to add to your Intentional Backpack. They're vital for your marriage, helping you to prioritize your relationship and keep it strong. They also help to rekindle romance in your marriage. And because you walk away refreshed, it's a win for all.

Bonus: Date Night Ideas

1. A trip down memory lane date: Do you remember your first dates with your husband? On this date, try to recreate those times. If you still live in the same area, go to places you went when you were dating. Create new memories at the places you used to go.

Jonathan and I moved away after we got married, so we improvise. In college, we often went to Fazoli's on our dates. We also enjoyed the coffeehouse in our college town. So on our trips down memory lane, we often hang out at Fazoli's or a local coffee shop.

2. Goodwill date: To begin this date, go out to eat. After dinner, head to a Goodwill store and choose outfits for each other. Try them on and then purchase the outfits for one another. Make sure you get pictures of one another in your "new" outfits.

3. Dollar date: To begin this date, go out to dinner and then head to a dollar store. Spend ten or fifteen minutes looking around. Find an item you like, and when the time is up, meet up again. Next, your husband needs to figure out what you want. As he gets closer to the item, tell him he is getting hot or hotter, and if he's far from it, say "cold" or "colder." Eventually, he will figure out what item you chose. Then it's your turn to figure out what your spouse wants. After playing the hot-and-cold game, buy the items for each other.

4. Blindfolded eating date: To begin this date, go to the grocery store together and secretly choose five to seven foods. You can pick items you know your spouse would love and/or hate. Purchase your items and head home. There, blindfold your husband and give him one of the foods you chose for him. Then he needs to guess what it is. Go through all the foods you chose, then it's your turn to be fed a mystery food. Have fun trying the foods! But keep a garbage can and glass of water close by.

Night-Out Ideas for Single Moms

Single moms need time away too, so please make sure to take time to care for yourself. You will be a better mom for being refreshed and refueled. If your family lives in town, consider asking your parents or sister to watch your child so you can get this time away. Another option is to ask a friend to watch your children and then watch her children her another time. You could also hire a trusted babysitter. Here are a few ideas of things you can do on your night out:

1. Go out to dinner, dessert, or coffee with friends, depending on your budget for the month. Enjoy this time connecting with one friend or a group of friends. Try new foods or coffee flavors.

2. Go to a canvas painting night. Take some friends along and enjoy this time together. Or if you would rather, go by yourself. Have fun getting creative!

3. Host a game night with your friends at your home. Pool your money for a babysitter to watch the kids. Have everyone bring a snack to share. Enjoy playing games other than Candyland or Uno.

4. Once or twice a year, grab some of your friends and get a hotel room, either in town or somewhere else. Split the cost and enjoy hanging out. Bring food along or plan to go out to eat. Enjoy a break from your mom tasks.

5. Host an evening at your home. Pool your money for a babysitter. Invite your friends to bring a snack and just hang out on your patio or deck. Take turns hosting so you can all enjoy getting out of the house.

———※———

Now let's take some time to reflect on the Bible verses below and decide on an action step for this chapter.

Then the Lord God said, "It is not good for the man to be alone. I will make a helper who is just right for him." So, the Lord God formed from the ground all the wild animals and all the birds of the sky. He brought them to the man to see what he would call them, and the man chose a name for each one. So the man gave names to all the livestock, the birds in the sky and all the wild animals. But for Adam no suitable helper was found. So, the Lord God caused the man to fall into a deep sleep; and while he was sleeping, he took one of the man's rib and then closed up the place with flesh. Then the Lord God made a woman from the rib he had taken out of the man, and he brought her to the man. "At last!" the man exclaimed. "This one is bone from my bone, and flesh from my flesh! She will be called 'woman,' because she was taken from 'man.'" This explains why a man leaves his father and mother and is joined to his wife, and the two are united into one. (Genesis 2:18–24)

Adam was assigned by God to name all the livestock, all the birds of the sky, and all the wild animals. Once he'd finished, Adam realized there was still not a helper just right for him. I love what God did next. It's so beautiful! He caused Adam to fall into a deep sleep. And then He took a rib and made a woman.

When Adam woke up, he realized that God had created a helper who was just right for him. He even sang a song about her in verse 23. In verse 24, God makes it clear that a man must leave his father and mother to join his wife and become one with her. The marriage relationship must take priority over all other relationships, other than each spouse's relationship with God. What a beautiful design! When we walk in this design, our marriages will thrive.

Pack Your Backpack: Choose One Action Step
1. Schedule a time to sit down with your spouse and look at the calendar.
2. Schedule one date night for next month. (Feel free to do more, but it's often better to start small and then build.)
3. Schedule one weekend getaway for the year.
4. Talk with the grandparents or adopted grandparents about keeping your kids for your weekend getaway.
5. Make a list of trusted friends to approach about date-night swapping and weekend getaways. Or find a trusted babysitter to pay each week for your date night.
6. Call one friend on this list and set up a date night for each family.

———※———

Before reading Genesis 2:18–24 below, ask the Holy Spirit to reveal something new to you through the verses.

Then the Lord God said, "It is not good for the man to be alone. I will make a helper who is just right for him." So the Lord God formed from the ground all the wild animals and all the birds of the sky. He brought them to the man to see what he would call them, and the man chose a name for each one. So the man gave names to all the livestock, the birds in the sky and all the wild animals. But for Adam no suitable helper was found. So the Lord God caused the man to fall into a deep sleep; and while he was sleeping, he took one of the man's ribs and then closed up the place with flesh. Then the Lord God made a woman from the rib he had taken out of the man, and he brought her to the man. "At last!" the man exclaimed. "This one is bone from my bone, and flesh from my flesh! She will be called 'woman,' because she was taken from 'man.'" This explains why a man leaves his father and mother and is joined to his wife, and the two are united into one. (Genesis 2:18–24)

1. In Genesis 2:20, we read that Adam still had no helper. What did God do about this?

_____

_____

_____

2. What does Adam realize in Genesis 2:23?

_____

_____

_____

_____

3. What must the husband do when he gets married? A wife also needs to do this.

_____

_____

_____

_____

4. Why do you think this is hard for some spouses?

_____

_____

_____

_____

5.   God designed marriage to be an exclusive, inseparable relationship between a man and woman. Does your marriage reflect this design? Why or why not?

_____

_____

_____

_____

Gentle Challenge

This chapter is about your number one relationship (under God), which should be your spouse. Take some time to ask the Lord if this is the case in your marriage, or whether your kids or other things have taken first place over your relationship with your spouse. Spend time journaling and asking God what you can do about this.

Encouragement

Date nights are not only important for your marriage relationship, but they are also important for your kids. Date nights communicate to your children that your marriage is the priority. Children also feel more secure when they see their parents together. Sit down with your spouse and find ways to work together to make date nights a priority.

Let's Pray

Dear God, thank you for the gift of my spouse. Please help me to keep my relationship with you my first priority and my marriage second. Holy Spirit, when I start to put other people or things ahead of my spouse, please convict me and remind me of your design for marriage. Please help us to take time to invest in our marriage, using date nights and weekend getaways. May we always keep you at the center of our marriage. In Jesus' name, amen.

Please write your own prayer here:

_____

_____

_____

_____

Journal

_____

_____

_____

_____

_____

_____

_____

_____

_____

_____

_____

_____

_____

_____

_____

_____

_____

_____

_____

_____

_____

_____

_____

_____

_____

_____

_____

_____

_____

CHAPTER 4
Marriage Habits

⎯⎯•◦◉◦•⎯⎯

*As the church submits to Christ, so you wives should submit to
your husbands in everything. For husbands, this means love
your wives, just as Christ loved the church.*

Ephesians 5:24–25

When I was a girl, lying in bed at night, I often tried to block out the noise by covering my ears. Tears soaked my pillow as I cried myself to sleep while my parents fought downstairs. I am not sure I always knew what they fought about. But I knew I could count on them fighting.

My siblings and I sometimes gathered in one of our rooms to console one another as we listened to the fighting. I am the third of eight children: five girls and three boys. As a child, I lived in two states and ten houses and went to at least nine schools, all before my sophomore year in high school. I spent second grade in two schools and two states.

We moved around a lot since we could never afford to buy a house. My mom stayed home with us kids. When we lived in Michigan for four and a half years, my dad attended the University of Michigan. I think he also had a job, but I honestly don't remember. The fighting was the worst when we lived in Ohio. My dad worked in a building in downtown Cleveland. I don't remember his exact job.

My family went to church, more from duty and obligation than out of a relationship with Jesus. The denomination I grew up in taught us that we had to earn our way to heaven. I know our home would have looked a lot different had my parents had a personal relationship with Jesus.

I grew up in a home where my parents didn't speak kind words to each other. This helped me to see how words impact the marriage relationship. In this chapter we'll look at five different habits to implement in marriage. We'll also discuss why each habit will be good for your marriage. You can add each of these habits to your Intentional Backpack.

Prayer

The first habit that will build a stronger marriage is praying together every day—in the morning, evening, or both. Couples need this time of prayer together because it connects us to the ultimate source of strength and wisdom: God.

Prayer is recognizing you need God and can't do it alone. It puts God at the center of your marriage, which strengthens it. Every morning, Jonathan and I ask each other what we can pray about for the day. We share our challenges and pray for the needs of the day—for example, wisdom, peace, and strength.

There is power in prayer. It is one of our greatest weapons, and we need to use it every day. I encourage you to add an extended time of prayer into your Intentional Backpack. Choose an evening during the week or a weekend for this extended time of prayer. Spend this extra time praying for your personal needs and for those of your children, family members, etc. Soon this will become a weekly routine that you'll look forward to.

I encourage you to begin your prayer time by praising God for who He is and all the ways He has answered your prayers. Read through your blessing book together (chapter 2).

You can also focus your prayer time by fasting together. Fasting involves going without food or other pleasant things for a period of time. It is a way to humble ourselves before God and seek His face. When we go without something, we're forced to turn to God and pray. It deepens our relationship with God and each other.

First, decide what you will fast from and narrow down your prayer focus. Maybe you have a big decision to make and could use some guidance.

Or maybe your marriage is struggling, and you want to focus on healing prayer. Fasting together is powerful. It will deepen your relationship with God and each other. We usually end the day with prayer.

If you are a single parent, I encourage you to pray with a trusted friend. Ask your pastor to connect you with a prayer partner. An older mom may be a great prayer partner.

Read the Bible Together

The second habit for a stronger marriage is reading the Bible together. Bible reading connects our hearts with God's truth. Reading the Bible helps us hear God's voice and learn how to be more like Him. This also strengthens your marriage.

Jonathan and I have used many devotionals over the years. Here are a few we have used:

> *Moments Together for Couples* by Dennis and Barbara Rainey
> *Draw Close* by Willard and Joyce Harley
> *My Utmost for His Highest* by Oswald Chambers
> *15 Minute Devotions for Couples* by Bob and Emilie Barnes

We have also used a Bible reading plan from the YouVersion app. Going deeper in God's Word connects you with your spouse in a powerful way.

Find a devotional book or Bible reading plan you both like. Spend time in God's Word together, and your marriage will grow stronger.

Couch Time

The third habit for a stronger marriage, which you can add to your Intentional Backpack, is couch time. Jonathan and I were introduced to the concept of "couch time" when we took the parenting class Growing Kids God's Way by Gary and Anne Ezzo. This is a focused time to sit together on the couch when you are both home, usually at the end of the work day.

During this time, talk about your days. This is a great way to connect with one another after a full day. Couch time is for just the two of you.

Train your kids not to bother you during this time. It takes time to train them, but your marriage is worth it.

Remind your kids that this is Mommy and Daddy time. Of course, it would be much easier to have couch time after the kids are in bed, but the key is letting the kids see you. Couch time helps children to feel more secure because they see you together.

One of our children can become extra needy and whiny at times. Often, this it is because they don't see Jonathan and me connecting enough. When we become more consistent with couch time, it's amazing how much this child changes. It is also a blessing for our marriage relationship. I feel more connected to my husband when we discuss our day. When we don't get this time, it's harder for us to feel connected in our intimacy.

Try to spend five to fifteen minutes talking on the couch. We often ask each other these questions: What was a high from today? What was your low or what challenge did you face today? We also talk about events that happened that day. It's also a good time to catch each other up on what is happening the rest of the evening.

How do you start couch time? First, call a family meeting and explain to your kids what couch time is and why it's important. If your kids are younger, you can explain it in simpler terms. After talking about it, have couch time for at least five minutes. It will take several days to train your kids not to bother you. When they talk to you during couch time, just calmly and politely remind them, "This is Mommy and Daddy's time. We will be available to talk to you in about _____ minutes."

We have found that it works to give attention and hugs to our kids just before we start couch time. We let them know we are starting, and then we give them time for one more question. As mentioned above, start with about five minutes. Slowly add minutes to your couch time until you are up to fifteen minutes or more.

Speak Highly of Your Spouse

The fourth habit for a stronger marriage to add to your Intentional Backpack is always speaking highly of your spouse. Not just sometimes, but all the time. And especially when you're experiencing conflict.

Don't run to your friends or parents and complain about your spouse. It's not beneficial or kind. Instead, when you need advice, go to one or two trusted people. As you share, always speak highly of your spouse. Focus on what you can do to help the problem, not on what they should do.

Also, when you're in public with your spouse, speak highly of them. Compliment your spouse, brag on them, but never put them down or complain about what they did wrong.

One way to speak highly of your husband is to post about him on social media. Think of specific examples and ways that your husband influences others' lives. Write up a post expressing your thanks. This is especially meaningful if your spouse's love language is words of affirmation.

If you don't want to post on social media, write him a thank-you note, complimenting him on the ways he blesses others. Or, instead of writing a note, simply tell him. All too often, we notice good things our spouse does, but we forget to mention them. Let this be the day we remember to praise our husbands.

One more way to speak highly of your husband is in your own mind. Have you ever heard your husband say something and then you reacted because of what you thought he meant? I wish I could say I don't react negatively to my husband, but I would be lying. All too often, I assume I know what Jonathan means, but in reality, I don't.

So I challenge you (and myself) to assume the best of your husband. When a conflict comes up in a conversation, choose to believe your husband has good intentions. Don't assume you know what he is thinking. Ask clarifying questions if needed. And remember, ask God for help in this. He is always for your marriage!

Single parents, this applies to you as you speak about your ex-spouse. Don't go to your friends or parents and complain about your ex-spouse. It's not beneficial or kind. As with married parents, discuss any problems with one or two trusted friends. Always speak highly of your ex-spouse. Focus on what you can do to help the problem, not on what they should do.

Also, when you are with your kids, always speak highly of their mom or dad, even if their actions make you think they don't deserve it. Never put them down or complain about what they did wrong in front of your children. This damages their relationship with you and their other parent.

Make Sex a Priority

The fifth habit for a stronger marriage to add to your Intentional Backpack is to make sex a priority. If I asked you, "What is your husband's number one need?" your answer would most likely be sex. Often this is a hard topic to talk about, but it's important. In fact, a whole book of the Bible is dedicated to sex. The Song of Solomon causes you to blush a lot, but it's a beautiful picture of God's design for sex.

God designed sex to be a beautiful experience between a husband and wife. It brings God great joy when He sees married couples have sex. That may sound a little weird, but it's true. If you aren't excited about having sex with your husband or just don't feel like having sex because you're too tired, I encourage you to pray about it. We women don't desire sex as much as our husbands do. But God can help us be available for our husbands and even enjoy that time with them.

It's very important to have a lock on your bedroom door. This keeps the kids out and guards your time with your spouse. Over the years, we have found that scheduling sex is helpful. The demands of family life and activities can take over if we let them. We learned to make sex a priority by scheduling it.

It may sound legalistic or odd, since people often think sex should be fun and spontaneous. Sex can still be fun, even when you schedule it. You'll sometimes have spontaneous sex too. We simply knew we needed to make sure sex happened, so scheduling it is a way to make it a priority.

Bonus: Challenge

Your challenge for today is for you and your husband to plan a romantic evening with sex. This challenge may take more than just a day, so take as much time as you need to plan. Or if you can pull it together for tonight, by all means, do so! I know your husband will love it.

Some ideas for your romantic evening include:

- Make your spouse's favorite dinner, served by candlelight
- Buy some new lingerie
- Create a treasure hunt in which your husband finds you in your bedroom
- Dance to love songs and seeing where it leads you
- Give each other a massage
- Take a bath together

One at a Time

One thing I really love about marriage is that we always have room to grow. Jonathan and I are still working on these habits. The past twenty-plus years have been a blessing because we have implemented these habits.

Which of the five habits jumped out at you? I encourage you to choose one habit to work on at a time. Once you have mastered it by at least 80 percent, move on to the next one. Here's to a stronger marriage, using the habits of prayer, Bible reading, couch time, speaking highly of one another, and making sex a priority.

———◦○◦———

And further, submit to one another out of reverence for Christ. For wives, this means submit to your husbands as to the Lord. For a husband is the head of his wife as Christ is the head of the church. He is the Savior of his body, the church. As the church submits to Christ, so you wives should submit to your husbands in everything. For husbands, this means love your wives, just as Christ loved the church. He gave up his life for her to make her holy and clean, washed by the cleansing of God's Word. He did this to present her to himself as a glorious church without a spot or wrinkle or any other blemish. Instead, she will be holy and without fault. In the same way, husbands ought to love their wives as they love their own bodies. For a man who loves his wife actually shows love for himself. After all, no one ever hated their own body, but they feed and care for their body, just as Christ does the church—for we are members of his body. "For this reason a man will leave his father and mother and be united to his wife, and the two will become one flesh." This is a profound mystery—but I am talking about Christ and the church. However, each one of you also must love his wife as he loves himself, and the wife must respect her husband. (Ephesians 5:21–33)

Marriage is a beautiful gift for us, ordained by God. But that doesn't mean it's easy. Too often, we have problems in our marriage because we don't live by God's design. These Scripture verses are packed with powerful truth, even though they may be hard to swallow. *Submission* is not most women's favorite word. I think for many of us, that's because we don't understand the true meaning. Let's unpack *submission* and *headship* and get a better grasp of submission.

As stated in Ephesians 5:21, we are to submit to one another out of reverence for Christ. Whether or not we agree with our husbands, God has asked us to submit to them out of reverence for Christ. Submission can be a beautiful thing because we honor our Lord. It's an amazing calling. If God asks us to submit to our husbands, He will supply what we need to submit. When we submit, we not only honor God, but we also affirm our husband in his leadership.

Once we understand the beauty of headship, it also becomes easier to submit. God has called husbands to love their wives as Christ loves the church. That's a tall order, but husbands can do it because God will give them what they need to succeed in loving their wives. In these Scripture verses, we see that a husband is to lead, protect, and provide for his family. God has ordained this design, and we are to trust it.

We wives need to stay under this leadership. To help us understand, let's picture an umbrella. As the leader of the family, the husband holds the umbrella of protection over the family. When we step out from under an umbrella and into the rain, we get soaked. When we step out from under the figurative umbrella, we leave our husband's protection. Even more serious, we step outside God's protection. Ladies, don't do this! Stay under God's ordained leadership. Trust Him.

Pack Your Backpack: Choose One Action Step

1. Start by praying with your spouse once a day, either in the morning or evening.
2. Choose a devotional or Bible reading plan to read with your spouse.
3. Call a family meeting and explain to your kids what couch time is and why you are going to do it.
4. Decide always to speak highly of your spouse and ask a friend to hold you accountable.
5. Brag on your husband on social media and when you're out with friends.
6. Plan a romantic evening for your spouse. Pick one of the ideas listed, or plan your own.

———※———

And further, submit to one another out of reverence for Christ. For wives, this means submit to your husbands as to the Lord. For a husband is the head of his wife as Christ is the head of the church. He is the Savior of his body, the church. As the church submits to Christ, so you wives should submit to your husbands in everything. For husbands, this means love your wives, just as Christ loved the church. He gave up his life for her to make her holy and clean, washed by the cleansing of God's Word. He did this to present her to himself as a glorious church without a spot or wrinkle or any other blemish. Instead, she will be holy and without fault. In the same way, husbands ought to love their wives as they love their own bodies. For a man who loves his wife actually shows love for himself. After all, no one ever hated their own body, but they feed and care for their body, just as Christ does the church—for we are members of his body. "For this reason a man will leave his father and mother and be united to his wife, and the two will become one flesh." This is a profound mystery—but I am talking about Christ and the church. However, each one of you also must love his wife as he loves himself, and the wife must respect her husband. (Ephesians 5:21–33)

Please read Ephesians 5:21–33 again. Before reading, ask the Holy Spirit to reveal something new to you. After reading, please answer the study questions below.

1. What does God ask both the husband and wife to do?

_____

_____

_____

_____

2. How are wives to submit to their husbands? Why are they to submit?

_____

_____

_____

_____

3. How did Jesus show His love for the church?

_____

_____

_____

4. How are husbands to love their wives?

_____

_____

_____

5. According to Ephesians 5:33, what must the wife do?

_____

_____

_____

_____

Gentle Challenge

Spend time with God and ask Him which habit to focus on strengthening this week: prayer, reading the Bible together, couch time, speaking highly of your spouse, or making sex a priority.

Encouragement
Implementing these five marriage habits will take time. Choose one habit at a time and focus on it for a week or two. Once you feel you have 80 percent success, move on to another habit. Take note and see how this strengthens your marriage.

Let's Pray
Dear God, thank you for the gift of my spouse. Lord, I want our relationship to be stronger. Please help us to make time to pray and read the Bible together. Your Word is alive and active, so I know it will strengthen us. God, I need your help in speaking highly of my spouse. No matter what he does or how he acts, may I always believe the best and speak highly of him. Thank you for being for our marriage, God. In Jesus' name, amen.

Please write your own prayer here:

_____
_____
_____
_____

Journal

_____
_____
_____
_____
_____
_____
_____
_____
_____
_____
_____
_____
_____

PART THREE

Parenting: Consistency and Variety with Unique Children

CHAPTER 5
Know Your Children

———◆———

When Jesus saw what was happening, he was angry with his
disciples. He said to them, "Let the children come to me. Don't
stop them! For the Kingdom of God belongs to those who are
like these children."

Mark 10:14

My childhood nickname was Goody Two Shoes. Let's be real right up front. I was not a golden child by any means. I talked back to my parents, lied, hurt my siblings, and didn't always follow through with what my parents asked me. But somehow, I still got that nickname. As I mentioned before, I am third in a family of eight children—three boys and five girls. How my mom survived is still a mystery to me, especially when she had several teenage girls at once.

As one of eight children and one who didn't act out a lot, I got lost in the shuffle. I know my parents did the best they could. But I did not grow up with much attention. I didn't feel noticed or seen. Over the years, a few teachers made me feel loved and important. However, as a child I decided to do all that I could to help my children feel known and loved.

How do we get to know our children? How do we make sure they feel loved and seen? In this chapter we will dig into a few of the many ways to get to know your children.

Your Child's Love Language

One of the ways to help your child feel known is by discovering their love language. Gary Chapman wrote a book called *The Five Love Languages*. Chapman teaches how each person gives and receives love through quality time, gifts, physical touch, acts of service, or words of affirmation (some people relate to more than one of these "languages"). When children are younger, it is recommended to try to speak all of the love languages to them until you know what their primary language is. Children need all these love languages spoken to them as they grow up.

But they do have a primary one that resonates with them. Do you know what that love language is? One way to figure out their love language is simply by observing your child. How do they express love to you? Ask your child what helps them feel loved. If your children are too young to answer this question, speak each of the love languages to them and see how they respond. For example, our oldest daughter, Micaela, doesn't receive hugs as well as our youngest, Caleb, does. He would hug you all day if you let him. Micaela prefers words of affirmation and gifts. Every child is different.

Here are a few ideas to help you figure out your child's primary love language:

Quality Time

- Your child will frequently ask to spend time with you.
- Your child will want to help you cook or run errands just so they can be with you.
- Your child loves to play board games or watch a movie with you.

Gifts

- Your child loves to receive gifts. They make a big deal about it.
- Your child loves when you surprise them with little gifts.
- Your child remembers the gifts given to them.
- Your child loves to give gifts.

Physical Touch

- Your child likes physical games, like wrestling, playing tag, or racing.
- Your child frequently grabs your hand or leans in to you.
- Your child loves to snuggle, cuddle, and be close to you.

Acts of Service

- Your child loves when you help them do something.
- Your child always wants to help and will do chores without being asked.
- Your child loves when you make them a favorite meal or dessert.

Words of Affirmation

- Your child is motivated by your words of encouragement.
- Your child likes to show you what they did and hear your opinion.
- Your child is sensitive to harsh words and criticism.
- Your child speaks encouragement and love to others.

Author Gary Chapman provides a test on his website to help you figure out your child's love language. If your kids are old enough, they can take the test on their own. Or if they are younger, you can read through the test with them. When you've learned your child's primary love language, it's time to speak it.

Here are a few ideas for love language activities to do with your child. Remember, each kid is different. If one of the ideas doesn't go over well with your child, try another one.

Quality Time

- Ask your child to pick out a board game to play with you.
- Take your child to a coffee shop or out to eat. Implement the no-screens rule so you can focus on one another.

- Have a pillow talk every night at bedtime. Invite your child to talk about their day.
- Keep a journal together. Write letters to one another.
- Get creative together. Look up crafts or projects you could do together.

Gifts

- Hide small gifts around the house and have a treasure hunt.
- Buy them a new outfit. Wrap it in pretty paper so they get to open it.
- Make your child's favorite meal or dessert. Or surprise them and bring home food from their favorite restaurant.
- Surprise them with tickets to an event they want to attend.
- Buy your child a toy they have been wanting.

Physical Touch

- Have a daily cuddle time on the couch. Read a book or watch a movie.
- Create a family handshake for greetings and goodbyes.
- Give a lingering hug every day. Make sure to hold for an extra moment or two.
- Hold their hand (younger kids) when you're out shopping together.
- Give your child a shoulder massage when they look worried or feel stressed.

Acts of Service

- Make your child's favorite breakfast once in a while, especially on a school day.
- Do one of your kid's chores for them.
- Go to a neighbor's house with your child and ask how you can help. Serve together.
- Make dinner together.

- Surprise your child by cleaning their room for them.

Words of Affirmation

- Write them an encouraging note and put it in their lunch box.
- Send a text to your child, letting them know what you appreciate about them. Or when they get home that day from school, pull them aside and share what you appreciate about them.
- Make a sign with your child's name on it, then wave it and cheer for them at their sporting events.
- When your children bring home test papers, write notes on them stating, "You did a good job" or "Well done."
- Write a note and tell your child five reasons why you love them. This is also something you can say out loud to them. Just make sure you have their attention before talking.

Questions to Ask Your Children

Another way to get to know your children is to ask them questions. Once a week, or more if you are able, spend time with your child and ask the questions below. Choose a few from the list, but be sure not to do them all at once so you don't overwhelm your child. These questions can help you understand your child more.

- On a scale of one to ten, how would you rate your day and why?
- What new fact did you learn today?
- What did you do today to make God smile?
- What did you do today that made you feel brave?
- How did you help someone today?
- What did I do today to make you feel loved?
- What did I do today that bothered you?
- What one thing can I do differently to be a better mom (dad) to you?
- What was the most fun part of your day?
- How do you feel right now? Are you worried about anything?

Ways to Pray Specifically for Your Kids

Another way to help your child feel known is by praying for them. We can pray for our kids in many ways. In this section, we'll discuss specific ways to pray. Each child has a character quality they need to develop. Once you've identified that area, work with your child to find a Scripture verse related to the growth point. Encourage your child to memorize that Scripture verse. Memorize it with them.

Each week, sit with your child and talk about the Scripture verse and how it can help them move toward the area they need to grow in. For example, at some point, each of our children has struggled with lying. At that time, we focused on what God's Word says about lying. We pulled out a Scripture verse to memorize, like this one: "The LORD detests lying lips, but he delights in those who tell the truth" (Proverbs 12:22).

We asked our child what the verse meant and how we could live it out. We encouraged our child to write out the Scripture verse to help them memorize it. Once they memorized the Scripture verse and we felt they had 80 percent success with this growth point, we moved on to another growth point.

Praying Hands

To pray specifically for your child's growth points, pick one Scripture verse to pray over them daily each day of the year. The Scripture should speak to who they are, what they struggle with, or what they need to grow in.

My husband and I spend time praying about which Scripture verses would strongly impact our children's life. Before our children were saved, we prayed a Scripture verse over them about salvation. We used a combination of Romans 10:9 and Romans 10:13.

Our older children were believers when we started this prayer journey. So we asked God for a specific verse for Micaela and Nathan. Both times, God made it clear what Scripture verse He wanted us to pray.

We used *Praying the Scriptures for Your Children* by Jodie Berndt to help us choose verses. This book breaks down the Scriptures in categories. It even has Scripture verses to pray over your adult children.

Once we decided on a Scripture verse for each child, I traced their hands onto sturdy paper and wrote their personalized Scripture verse on it. I like to do this on January 1 or close to the beginning of the year. It has been an amazing tool and a great visual for both Jonathan and me. We share the verse with the child so they know how we are praying for them. This is a way to pour into them and show them that we care about their growth in God.

Stop, Look, and Listen

One other way to know our children is to stop, look, and listen regularly. My kids love to tell me about a book they are reading, a game they are playing, or what happened at a friend's house. They share so many details, I sometimes have a hard time tracking the point of their stories. To be totally honest, sometimes I get weary of listening.

My mind shifts to the messy kitchen I need to clean or the project I'm in the middle of. Sometimes I half-listen and keep working on whatever I was in the middle of. Does this describe you? Maybe just a little? The Holy Spirit has been stirring in my heart about my focus. He has been asking me to stop, look, and listen.

First, I need to be willing to stop what I'm doing and listen to my kids. They are sharing something that is very important to them; therefore, it's important to me. If I'm in the middle of something and can't stop, I try to respond in this way: "I would love to hear your story, but right now is not a good time. In about ten minutes (or whatever time needed), I can hear your story." This communicates to my kids that I value them.

Second, I need to look at my son or daughter when they speak to me—not above or behind them but right into their eyes. I admit this has been hard for me. My mind constantly races with thoughts of everything I need to do. Looking has been hard, but it's been a good practice for me. Looking at someone in the eye shows respect and communicates value. My kids are extremely valuable to me, so I'm going to keep working on looking at them.

As I look into my child's eyes, I also need to listen, and not half-heartedly. How many times have I half-listened to my kids while thinking about dinner prep or the clothes waiting in the washer? Too many times. As I practice fully listening to my kids, I'll get to know them better.

I have a long way to go on this journey. It is hard to stop, look, and listen. I'm thankful the Holy Spirit has convicted me in this area. My kids aren't going to be young forever. These years are going way too fast. When my kids look back on their childhood, I want them to remember that their mom took time to stop, look, and listen.

Without a shadow of doubt, I want my kids to know they are valuable and loved more than my projects and long to-do list. How about you? Where is your focus when your child speaks to you? I encourage you to stop, look, and listen. I think you will be surprised at what you learn.

The Power of Words

I'm a people watcher, especially at restaurants. In line one day at a fast-food restaurant, I observed a mom with her three children. Every word that came from her mouth was negative and tore her kids down. My heart broke for these kids as I watched them shrink down in their booth. One of them wanted to sit outside, but the mom yelled loudly enough for everyone there to hear, "We will not sit outside!" I'm not sure what was going on with this mom, but it didn't warrant this behavior.

Unfortunately, I have had these moments of acting out in frustration at my kids. Not in public for all to hear, but in our home. I feel terrible afterward and wish I could retract every word. The Holy Spirit lovingly convicts me in these moments. I confess my sin to God. Then I go and find my child and ask for their forgiveness too.

I heard author and speaker Kevin Leman comment that when you yell at your kids, you basically throw up all over them. I don't know about you, but I personally don't want to throw up on my kids.

The words we speak to our kids matter more than we realize. If we find ourselves feeling frustrated like the mom from the story, we need to take a deep breath and keep our mouths shut.

In Proverbs 10:11, we read, "The words of the godly are a life-giving fountain; the words of the wicked conceal violent intentions." We want our words to give life to our kids. "The tongue can bring death or life; those who love to talk will reap the consequences" (Proverbs 18:21).

In Galatians 5:16, we read, "So I say, walk by the Spirit, and you will not gratify the desires of the flesh." When we are struggling with our words, because those days do happen, we must rely on the Lord to help us. The Holy Spirit lives in us so He can help us to have self-control. If we are struggling with self-control, we may just need to put ourselves in timeout. Our words need to bring life.

Last year, when I was riding the hotel elevator to the lobby, a boy dressed in a baseball uniform got in with a man. The boy referred to him as Dad, so I knew the father and son were headed to a baseball game. I love baseball, so I asked the boy what position he played.

He hesitated, his head down, as he stared at the floor. "Center field."

"Yes, Josh is really good at it," his dad said. "He's fast and accurate."

The dad's words poured confidence and courage into his son. Josh stood a little taller and looked ready to conquer that game. I wish I could have seen him play that day, because I'm sure nothing got past him. The words we speak to our kids and about our kids matter.

Three Things I Tell My Kids Every Day

My desire is to build up my kids and pour truth into them with my words, building their confidence. One way I do this is by telling my kids three things before they leave for the day.

First, I tell my kids, "You're strong." I want them to see themselves as having great strength because God has given it to them. I remind them of Joshua 1:9, in which God commanded Joshua to be strong and courageous. He also reminded Joshua that He was with them wherever they went. I remind my kids that they can be strong because God is with them.

Second, I tell my kids, "You're brave." I want them to know they can handle whatever comes their way because God is with them. We have read the story of David and Goliath countless times over the years. David was young, but he was brave. I remind my kids that they're like David and can conquer giants.

And finally, I tell my kids, "You're going to do great things for God today." I want them to know I believe in them and that I know they will reflect God in their actions. I want them to focus on serving God and loving others. This truth helps them to focus on serving God instead of themselves.

———⊙———

> Then they brought little children to Him, that He might touch them; but the disciples rebuked those who brought them. But when Jesus saw it, He was greatly displeased and said to them, "Let the little children come to Me, and do not forbid them; for of such is the kingdom of God. Assuredly, I say to you, whoever does not receive the kingdom of God as a little child will by no means enter it." And He took them up in His arms, laid His hands on them, and blessed them. (Mark 10:13–16 NKJV)

I love the parents' boldness in these Scripture verses. They knew who Jesus was and wanted their children to know too. They even pushed through the disciples' opposition. The disciples were just trying to do their job. Little did they know what Jesus had in store to teach them. Jesus was displeased with His disciples, and rightfully so. They had disregarded children and treated them like an interruption.

In the culture of that day, children had no social status. By telling the disciples to let the children come to Him, Jesus communicated these children's value. He also encouraged others to be like them. Children have a faith in God that adults need to take note of and imitate. Children also depend on God in a beautiful way. When we have this kind of faith, we are more ready to receive God into our lives.

Pack Your Backpack: Choose One Action Step
1. This week, schedule time to ask your children a few of the connection questions listed in this chapter.
2. Discover your child's primary love language. Pick one day this week and be intentional in speaking their love language. Slowly build up to speaking their love language daily.

3. Choose a Scripture verse to pray over your child each day of this year. You can start any time of the year.

4. Stop, look, and listen each time your child talks to you. Take note of how your child responds.

5. Grab a notebook and write down at least five things you said to your child that day. Evaluate your words. Did they build up or tear down your child? If your words tore down your child at all, confess that sin to God. And then also ask your child for forgiveness. This will go a long way in building a healthy relationship with your child.

6. Think of three things to tell your kids every day. Feel free to use my examples. Be sure to communicate them daily.

———— ⚬⊛⚬ ————

> Then they brought little children to Him, that He might touch them; but the disciples rebuked those who brought them. But when Jesus saw it, He was greatly displeased and said to them, "Let the little children come to Me, and do not forbid them; for of such is the kingdom of God. Assuredly, I say to you, whoever does not receive the kingdom of God as a little child will by no means enter it." And He took them up in His arms, laid His hands on them, and blessed them. (Mark 10:13–16 NKJV)

Please read Mark 10:13–16. Before reading, ask the Holy Spirit to reveal something new to you. After reading, please answer the study questions below.

1. How can you bring your children to Jesus?

_____

_____

_____

_____

2. The disciples scolded the parents for bringing them to Jesus. How often do you unnecessarily scold your children without realizing it?

_____

_____

_____

3. Why was Jesus displeased with his disciples?

_____

_____

_____

_____

4. Why is it important to have childlike faith?

_____

_____

_____

_____

5.   From the following list, choose one Scripture verse to pray over your children as a way to bless them.

- 1 Peter 5:8
- Philippians 4:8
- Proverbs 3:5–6
- Isaiah 26:3
- Joshua 1:9

Gentle Challenge

In this chapter we talked about stopping, looking, and listening. Take a moment and ask God how you're doing with this skill. If you're struggling to stop, look, and listen, ask God to help you the next time your child comes to tell you something. Use a sticky note to write the words "Stop, look, and listen" as a reminder to implement this strategy.

Encouragement

Spend time studying your children. Learn what makes them feel loved. Ask them questions. Use the love language test for kids to discover what helps your child feel as if you love them. Each day, express love in one way to each of your children, and see what a difference it makes.

Let's Pray

Dear God, thank you for the gift of my children. You have designed each one uniquely. Please teach me how to study my child(ren) and love them well. Lord, when they come to speak to me, please help me to speak love and acceptance in my words and actions. May my child(ren) always know how valuable and precious they are to me. Thank you for your guidance, Lord. In Jesus' name, amen.

Please write your own prayer here:

_____

_____

_____

_____

Journal

_____

_____

_____

_____

_____

_____

_____

_____

_____

_____

_____

_____

_____

_____

_____

_____

_____

_____

CHAPTER 6
Enjoying Your Children

————◆————

Children are a gift from the Lord; they are a reward from him.
Psalm 127:3

When I was a child, my dad was not home much because he worked a lot of late hours. I'm not sure why. It bothered my mom, my siblings, and me, but we learned to work with it. Every once in a while, Dad brought gifts home for us. My primary love language is gifts, so I loved that. But a part of me still ached because I wanted time with my dad, to have him notice me—to see and affirm changes in me.

But money can't buy love, and besides, children don't really want all the stuff. They're crying out for you to spend time with them and love them. And once we get to know our children better, we can't help but love and enjoy them more.

But do our kids know we enjoy them? This chapter will look at ways to enjoy our children, from special outings to simplifying family life. Then our children will know we treasure them.

One-on-One Time with Your Kids
What is your child's favorite color? What is their greatest fear? What kind of books do they like to read? We can learn the answers to these questions and many others by having individual time with our children.

One-on-one time is important because it communicates value to your kids. This time of individual attention tells your child they're worthy of quality time with you. Your presence with your child is one of the best gifts you could give them.

This presence is different from just being at home or at a ball game. In those settings, your child doesn't have your full attention, which is understandable. Spend time with your child when you can be fully engaged and present.

Another reason one-on-one time is important is because it builds your relationship with that individual child. Think about it. How did you get to know your best friend? By spending time with them.

One-on-one time with your children also helps you to see life from their perspective and get to know their preferences. This time gives you the opportunity to ask questions and engage with your children more.

Often, children will act up when they need attention. Does this happen in your home? Children figure some negative attention is better than no attention. We can answer this cry by intentionally spending time with them. Investing in our children will reduce negative behavior.

One-on-one time is a great idea and all, but how do we fit it in? By creating the time. Every family is different, so you'll need to figure out what works best for your current season of life. The length of time we spend with each individual child will vary. Ten or fifteen minutes a day or a couple of times a week invested in our children is priceless.

In our family, we created a schedule for one-on-one time and hung it on the refrigerator. Talk about accountability. The kids love knowing when they'll have their time with Mom. The posted schedule is also a great visual for me.

During the summer, my goal is to have time with the kids each day. During the school year, I try to have one day for each kid. Of course, I would love to do more. But in reality, things come up. Someone needs help with homework, our schedule changes, etc. That is why I try to be proactive and schedule at least one day, and if more time is available, I use it.

One-on-one time is important because it communicates value, builds relationships, and helps behavior. How can you work this into your family life? Below are some ideas. Feel free to use some or all of them.

If you are a single mom with several kids, have one of your older children watch the other kids if they are able. If not, team up with a friend or another mom. Another option is to ask your parents to watch the other kids while you spend time with one of your children.

One-on-One Time Ideas for Younger Kids (babies through age two)

- Take a walk
- Sit by a window with your child on your lap
- Read books to your child
- Watch a Baby Mozart or Praise Baby DVD together
- Blow bubbles inside or outside

One-on-One Time Ideas for Younger Kids (ages two through seven)

- Put together a puzzle
- Play a board game
- Play with play dough
- Color with the child
- Do a simple craft together

One-on-One Time Ideas for Older Kids (ages eight and up)

- Run errands with your child
- Take a walk around the block with your child
- Invite your child to help you cook dinner
- Take your child out for a special treat
- Play their favorite board game

One-on-One Outings with Mom and Dad

Our kids need to have individual time with both parents, but this can be hard to do. Jonathan and I were determined to make this work, so we got creative. Each month, our children get to go out with one of their parents.

On the first Sunday of the month, Jonathan and I take the girls out. Micaela goes with me, and Analiah goes with Jonathan. The following month, we take our other daughter. We have a budget line for these outings, so the kids each have some money to spend. The types of outings vary by the child.

Our older son (age fourteen) watches his brother. If your kids are too young to stay by themselves, consider swapping babysitting with a friend, or ask your parents to watch the other kids.

If you are a single parent, I also recommend that you take your kids out at least once a month. If the budget is tight, have simple outings or save for bigger ones. If you have multiple children, consider swapping with a friend or asking your parents to watch the kids.

One of my favorite outings was going to Martin's grocery store in their Side Door Deli. Analiah bought cucumbers from the salad bar. We also bought sparkling ice drinks. Analiah picked up a straw to go with her bottled drink. It was fun to watch her play with the straw as it bobbed up and down. The moment was silly but memorable as we sat on the tall chairs in Martin's Side Door Deli.

On the third Sunday of the month, Jonathan and I take out the boys. It's fun to see what they come up with for outings. Nathan's choice generally involves food. I often joke about food being a love language. Our kids look forward to this time, and we also enjoy the time to connect with them.

No-Screens Rule

It's easy for Jonathan and me to be distracted by our phones. Therefore, we have implemented a no-screens rule during our individual time with our kids. The rule is in place not to be legalistic, but to encourage connection. We want this to be a time when our kids have our full attention, so they will know they're more valuable than whatever is on our phones. It's also a great way to model to them how to connect with friends once they have their own phones.

Hug Your Kids

Giving a hug to your child communicates love and acceptance. I did not grow up in a physically demonstrative family, so it has been a challenge for me to be physical with my kids. However, I want them to feel loved and valued. Giving your child at least two to three if not more hugs each day is a way to enjoy your children. Hugging has many benefits too. Think about how a hug makes you feel when you are scared. Sometimes our children wake up with a bad dream. When they do, a hug goes a long way to help them feel safe and secure.

Hugs release oxytocin, which is often called the love hormone, in our brains. Oxytocin is known for reducing depression and anxiety. Every time you hug your child, you help them relieve stress.

When you hug your child, you also boost their self-confidence. The hug itself reassures our children that they are valuable and loved. Our hugs are like a safety net for our kids. They grow in loving who they are, which in turn helps them to love others.

A simple hug is more important for our children than we probably realize. This is an area I definitely need to grow in. God created hugs as a way to help us enjoy our kids more.

Read to Your Kids

Another way to enjoy our children is to read aloud to them, no matter their age. This sounds simple but has many benefits. First, you are spending time with your kids. You are getting to know their interests by reading several different types of books. You are learning what they enjoy.

Reading aloud also helps your kids to learn new vocabulary, increases their attention span, and builds comprehension of a story. These are all great benefits, especially when they start school.

Another benefit of reading to your kids is that holding them in your lap fills the child's physical-touch needs. As they get older, this is hard, but you can always sit close to them if they let you. Below is a list of read-aloud book possibilities.

For babies: Colorful board books with great pictures. Public libraries usually have a great selection.

For toddlers and preschool: picture books. Here are some titles:

The Elephant and Piggie series by Mo Willems
The Memory String by Eve Bunting
The Butterfly House by Eve Bunting
Chrysanthemum by Kevin Henkes
Lily's Purple Plastic Purse by Kevin Henkes
The Hungry Caterpillar by Eric Carle
Papa, Please Get the Moon for Me by Eric Carle
Thundercake by Patricia Polacco
Good Night Moon by Margaret Wise Brown

For elementary age: chapter books. These are some of our favorites:

The Chronicles of Narnia series by C. S. Lewis
Charlotte's Web by E. B. White
Stuart Little by E. B. White
The Boxcar Children by Gertrude Chandler Warner
Ramona series by Beverly Clearly
Ralph S. Mouse series by Beverly Clearly
Encyclopedia Brown, Boy Detective by Donald J. Sobol

Playing with Your Child

Playing with your child is another way to enjoy them. In the process, the child learns to interact with others in a loving and kind way. Playing with others also helps kids learn self-control as they wait their turn. And they'll learn how to react when things don't go their way.

While playing with you, your children will learn to be creative. You can use a cardboard box for many things. You can create a mailbox, write letters to the child, and pretend they are from all over the world. Or you can ask friends or family members from others states or countries write letters to your kids.

If you have a very large cardboard box, you can create a pretend house. This is a great way to model for your kids. Build spaces in which your child can be creative. Let them lead you on an adventure.

Playing with your children also helps them to learn gross motor skills. When you play outside, you are walking, throwing balls, kicking a soccer ball, or even running. Your children learn about speed and balance and become aware of their own strength. This is a great time to pour encouragement into them.

When you spend time with your kids, you communicate that they are valuable. Playing with your child builds your relationship and adds joy to your lives. Play is a place to work through hurts and disappointments together, which brings you closer. Playing with your child develops a stronger bond with your children.

Here are some ideas to get you started playing with your child.

- Play a game of tag, freeze tag, or even toilet tag. (Kids love this one! If they are tagged, they freeze in a squatting position with one arm out. The only way to get free is for someone to sit on them and flush the toilet, using their arm.)
- Create an obstacle course to go through together. Simplify or make it harder, depending on the children's ages.
- Blow bubbles. Use a fan to extend their reach.
- Throw a ball around.
- Four square. With every hit, share something you love about your children.
- Make up a story to tell your child, or make up a story together.

As you play together, you will connect with your kids' hearts and learn to enjoy them more.

Simplify Family Life

Have you simplified your family life? This is another way to enjoy our children more. However, it's not easy, since our culture promotes filling our calendars with many activities. First, we need to remember that we, the parents, are in charge of the family schedule. Our culture is not. Our kids' activities do not dominate our schedule.

Single moms, I can only imagine how full your life must be as you manage so many things on your own. I encourage you to talk with a trusted friend, mentor, or your parents and find ways you can simplify your family life to give you more breathing room.

How to Take Back Control of Your Calendar

First, we need to realize that we are in control of our calendars. Once we realize that, we remember that we are the only ones who can add or take things away from our calendar. We are the ones who decide how to spend our time as a family.

I have occasionally felt overwhelmed with our family schedule. When our oldest daughter was a freshman, she joined the cross-country team at the high school, and our second-oldest joined the football team at the middle school. Both practices ended at the same time. How in the world could we pick up the kids at the same time when Jonathan wasn't home from work? I'm sure all single parents can relate to this predicament.

There were times that Micaela had a cross-country meet on the same day Nathan had a football game. We had to divide and conquer. It felt very full at so many points. I had to remind myself to not complain. Why? Because we chose to do this. We made the decision to allow our kids to play sports. We made the decision to fill our calendar.

We did figure out ways to get our kids home from practice. It took a lot of juggling, but we got everyone home, even on the days one of the kids had to wait a little longer to be picked up. At times, we arranged for one child to ride home with a friend on the team. Single moms, if your parents are in the area, I encourage you to ask for their help. We don't have family nearby, so we had to rely on our friends.

Once we change our perspective and realize who is in charge of the schedule, we can enjoy our time more. When you look at your calendar, does it feel like too much? What have you added to your schedule that you need to let go of?

Another way to take back control of your calendar is to have an overview of the week and even the month. On Saturday or Sunday, take time to look at the week ahead. What commitments do you have? What is happening each night of the week? That way, when a friend asks to go out to coffee or your child asks to get together with a friend, you know what availability you have and don't have.

In our family, we try not to have too many full nights, especially during the school year. Occasionally, a Monday event comes up. When that happens, we switch our weekly date night to Thursday instead of Tuesday. That way, we are not gone two nights in a row. When you look ahead to the week, you can avoid overbooking yourself.

As a family, take time to look over your calendar for the next month. Look at the big picture and see what feels too full. What can you take out? These discussions are a great way for your children to learn how to manage their time. It also helps them express what they would like to do or not do in the coming month.

We choose to make church a priority every Sunday and Wednesday. Since our children were babies, we have been involved in midweek ministry. They started memorizing simple Scripture verses in their Wednesday-night class. They are always learning about God and worshipping Him, since we stayed involved in our church.

We also add church outreach activities to the calendar as they come up. Jonathan and I both serve in different ministries the church. We have encouraged our older two kids to get involved too. In the last couple of months, Micaela, our oldest, has been volunteering in the nursery. These are character-building activities to include in the calendar.

As we discussed in chapter 1, family fun nights are a great way to create meaningful memories and build confidence in your kids. Are family fun nights on your family calendar? If not, I encourage you to make those a priority.

Do Our Kids Know We Enjoy Them?

This is a tough question and one I always want my kids to answer with a loud "Yes!" I want to be that parent who thoroughly enjoys my children, no matter how they act or what they do. We can do this by having one-on-one times with our kids during the week. Monthly outings with Mom or Dad help our children to see we value time with them.

Other ways to enjoy our kids more is by taking time to hug them each day and by reading to them, even when they are older. Play is an important part of connecting with your child and learning to enjoy them. Simplifying your family calendar goes a long way in enjoying your kids.

You will all have breathing room and feel more peaceful, which in turn helps you to enjoy each other.

———◆———

> Children are a gift from the Lord; they are a reward from him. Children born to a young man are like arrows in a warrior's hands. How joyful is the man whose quiver is full of them! He will not be put to shame when he confronts his accusers at the city gates. (Psalm 127:3–5)

Psalm 127 begins with powerful verses that set us up for verses three through five. Psalm 127:1 reads, "Unless the Lord builds a house, the work of the builders is wasted. Unless the Lord protects a city, guarding it with sentries will do no good." This verse shows us that God blesses and protects His people. Without God, we will not be successful. Our efforts are wasted.

This verse points us to verses three through five. Children are a gift from the Lord. He uses them in our lives to bless us. In Hebrew, the words translated "children" (Hebrew *banim*) and "builders" (*bonim*, Psalm 127:1) are a wordplay. Having children builds a family. Isn't that a beautiful picture?

Our children are a gift from God. It may not always feel that way. In those moments, we need to ask God to help us enjoy our children. God promises to supply all our needs. So He will give us eyes to see our children the way He does. They are a blessing.

Pack Your Backpack: Choose One Action Step

1. Schedule a time to spend fifteen minutes with your child this week. Decide on an activity from the ideas above or think of your own.
2. Look over your calendar. Choose a day to take your child out for some one-on-one connecting time. Ask them what they would like to do.
3. Implement the no-screens rule when you are with your children.
4. Challenge yourself to hug your child at least three times today. Notice their response.
5. Choose one of the play ideas listed above and do it with your child. What did you discover about your child during play time?

6. Plan a family meeting to look over your calendar together. What can you take off your calendar? What do you want to add?

———◦◦◦———

> Children are a gift from the Lord; they are a reward from him. Children born to a young man are like arrows in a warrior's hands. How joyful is the man whose quiver is full of them! He will not be put to shame when he confronts his accusers at the city gates. (Psalm 127:3–5)

Please read Psalm 127:3–5. Before reading, ask the Holy Spirit to reveal something new to you. After reading, please answer the study questions below.

1. How are your children a gift from the Lord?

_____

_____

_____

2. How are children a reward from the Lord?

_____

_____

_____

3. Children are called arrows in our Scripture verses. Read Psalm 7:12–14 and Psalm 120:4. How are arrows used in these Scriptures?

_____

_____

_____

4. When a man has a full quiver of arrows, what is he like?

_____

_____

_____

_____

5. How do your children build up your family?

_____

_____

_____

_____

Gentle Challenge
In this chapter we learned about the importance of one-on-one time with our children. Do you are currently have these times? If not, what can you do this week to implement one-on-one time?

Encouragement
Do your family life and schedule feel out of control? If so, it's time to simplify your calendar. Reread the section about simplifying family life. Choose one of the strategies to implement in your family.

Let's Pray
Dear God, I want my children never to doubt their value and worth. I know how I treat them plays a big role in this. Lord, teach me to pour into my children so they know I enjoy them. Please help me to make it a priority to play with my children and hug them each day. Thank you, Holy Spirit, for your guidance in this all. In Jesus' name, amen.

Please write your own prayer here:

_____

_____

_____

_____

Journal

_____

_____

_____

_____

_____

_____

_____

_____

_____

_____

_____

_____

_____

_____

_____

_____

_____

_____

_____

_____

_____

_____

_____

_____

_____

_____

_____

_____

_____

PART FOUR

The Home: It's Not Just a Place, but a Feeling

CHAPTER 7
The Physical Environment of Your Home

But as for me and my household, we will serve the lord.
Joshua 24:15

While I was growing up, an average day in my home was filled with chaos. I am one of eight children, so there was always noise. Looking back, I realize that chaos contributed to my anxiety and stomachaches. In this chapter we will look at the environment of the home. Are our homes welcoming? Are they comfortable? Do they feel peaceful or chaotic? Let's take a look at some strategies that will help us create an encouraging environment.

Physical Home
When your walk into your home, does it feel inviting? Does it feel like a haven? How do you think it feels to your kids? The way our home is set up makes a big difference, no matter what size home we live in.

When we moved into our home a year and a half ago, we automatically put our large sectional couch in the main living room. It's a comfortable, inviting couch. But the room was too small for it, and the brown couch made it look crowded. Why? Because that living room is long but not wide. A sectional couch does not work in that type of room. We moved that couch into our basement because it fits that space.

We spent time looking for comfortable reclining couches to make the living room feel inviting to our family and guests. We feel more relaxed in that room, now that it has the correct couches.

Think about the spaces in your home. Does any room feel too crowded? When you walk in the room, do you feel peaceful or overwhelmed? Your kids will feel the same way.

Think about your kitchen or dining area. Is the table crammed into a small space? A smaller table may feel more comfortable. Or is there enough room around it to make you feel comfortable at the table? Think through your child's bedroom. Does it have too much furniture crammed in there? What can you pull out?

What room in your home makes your kids feel most comfortable? Do they go there to recharge and relax? What can you do to create a comfortable place for your kids?

If you do need to get rid of a larger table for a smaller one, I suggest talking with friends to see if anyone has a table they aren't using. Another option is to go to a thrift store to see what they have. Check online garage sales or in-person sales. If you want a different couch, I recommend doing the same thing. You could even swap with a friend who wants make changes in their home. You can be creative without spending much money.

Clear the Clutter

Now that you have taken a look at the furniture and how it is arranged in your home, let's talk about the clutter. Clutter can be constant in a home with children. But it doesn't have to take over. Clutter can drain us and consume our energy, so work together as a family to clear the clutter.

The first step in clearing the clutter is to get rid of big items, like furniture, to create more space. Then look for toys that your kids haven't used in years. Take an inventory. What items have you not used in years? What can you get rid of?

Recently, Jonathan and I cleaned out the basement storage closet. This storage closet is very large, with four sliding doors. It takes up one wall in our basement. I am embarassed to say that we lived in our home for over a year before we cleaned it out. When we moved, we shoved boxes into this closet. We also unpacked all our board games and put then on these shelves. Our children would shove board games back into the closet when they're done playing with them.

You can just imagine the mess the storage closet was. Dice strewn in many different places and card games scattered on the floor. Random game pieces in multiple places. Legos tossed into game boxes and shoved to the back of the closet. Every time I went downstairs, I avoided this area, since it taunted me and reminded me what a mess it was.

Several times, we planned to clean it out, but something more important always came up. Finally, we nailed down a date and pushed through cleaning the closet. It was quite a project but totally worth all the effort. We took two boxes to the thrift store. We threw away lots of things and moved some items to our craft room cupboard upstairs.

Do you need to go through a closet in your house and clear some clutter? Maybe the linen closet is one of those places. Do the towels jump out at you, or do the sheets fall down like a waterfall because they just got shoved in the cupboard? As a family, talk about the big clutter that needs to be cleared. Work together to clean it out. It will make a big difference.

Clearing the clutter day to day makes a big difference. Here are a few ideas to help clear the clutter in your home.

- Mail: Don't get the mail until you have a few minutes. Pull out the junk mail and recycle it. Then go through the rest and decide where it goes. Do you need to file something? Does a bill need to be paid? Take care of that right away.
- Kids' school papers: Create a bulletin board for your kids' papers or use your refrigerator. If they come home with artwork or a test they did great on, hang it up for a week. When the week is up, either recycle the paper or store it in a box of keepsakes.
- Laundry: This is a never-ending task, but you can conquer it. Make a plan that works for your family. It all depends on how often you do laundry. When the kids were younger, I planned a chunk of time to fold all the laundry at once. Now I don't fold as much, since the kids fold their own. But all too often, the clean, dry laundry

sits, and that is draining. Work with your family to come up with a plan. Single moms and moms of newborns, I give you permission to dress your babies or kids from the laundry basket. I can only imagine the things you need to keep track of, so it is totally okay to pull your child's clothes for the day from the laundry basket.

- Backpacks and sports bags: These can easily clutter your house if you let them. Make a routine of putting away the backpacks and other sports items as soon as the kids get home. Make sure you have hooks somewhere, whether in a closet or on the wall, for your kids to hang their coats on.

- Toys: There's always a never-ending supply, right? However, toys don't have to overtake your home. When our kids were younger, we rotated toys each month. Jonathan and I set out all the toys in the living room. Then we divided them into sets. One set was for the living room toy box, and we had a set of toys for each kid's room. We labeled each set A, B, or C. Each set contained toys for the living room toy box and for each child's room. Every month, we pulled out either set A, B, or C. It was a fun way to bring out "new" toys every month. It was also wonderful to not have toys everywhere.

Here are a few more decluttering ideas:

- Put things in their home: Teach your children that everything has a home. The home for your shoes is your closet. The home for your coat is the coat closet. The home for your library books is on the shelf. The home for the markers is the craft cupboard. Give items a home and encourage your kids to put them in their home each day.

- Weekly bedroom cleanout: Teach your kids to spend a certain amount of time every Saturday clearing out the clutter in their rooms. Teach your kids what clutter is. During the first few weeks, help them to declutter by showing them what to keep and what to get rid of. Often, children's "treasures" are clutter. They don't realize how much they have accumulated and not touched for weeks. That's why a weekly cleanout is a good idea for your kids.

- Schedule family declutter days: Once a quarter, schedule a declutter day on your family calendar. As a family, start with one room in the house. Look at the common clutter spots in each room and see what you can clear out. The bookshelf in our living room and the craft cupboard are two places we usually need to declutter because things just get shoved in sometimes. Do you remember our large basement closet? Areas like that in your home are another great place to declutter during this time. What are some of the more cluttered places in your home?

During the declutter days, spend time with your kids in their rooms. Have they outgrown any of their clothes? Do their dresser drawers overflow? Pull out the clothes the kids have outgrown and pass them on to a friend or thrift store. Throw away the holey socks. Do you need to find any missing library books? This is a great time to look. Are there any broken toys? How about toys and games your kids don't play with anymore? When you help them declutter their rooms, you teach them life skills. They also learn what is and isn't important to them.

Let the Sun Shine In!

Believe or not, the sun plays a big part in your home's environment. So let the sun shine in! The whole family will benefit from the vitamin D they'll get. Sunlight also adds brightness to the house and naturally brings joy. Children and parents are much more motivated to do things when it is bright. Being in a dark room can make us feel sleepy, down, and discouraged. So let that sun shine in!

Shhh! Quiet the Noise

The world around us is constantly on the move and filled with lots of noise. Our homes can tend to be that way too, especially when everyone is around. But we can intentionally quiet the noise.

Through the years, I have walked into many homes that have the TV on constantly, but nobody's watching it. The TV is on just for background noise. And this noise only adds to the noise of the house.

It's okay to have the TV on for background noise, but I highly recommend that we don't leave it on all the time. Choose a time in your day to have no extra noise and enjoy the quiet.

The physical environment of our home plays a big role in creating meaningful memories and building confidence in our kids. At the beginning of this section, I asked several questions. *When your walk into your home, does it feel inviting? Does it feel like a haven? How do you think it feels to your kids?* As you read through this last section, did some ideas make you stop and think? Do you see ways to create a more peaceful and calmer physical environment in your home?

But if serving the Lord seems undesirable to you, then choose for yourselves this day whom you will serve, whether the gods your ancestors served beyond the Euphrates, or the gods of the Amorites, in whose land you are living. But as for me and my household,we will serve the Lord. (Joshua 24:15)

The last part of Joshua 24:15 is one of the most quoted Bible verses: "'But as for me and my household, we will serve the Lord.'" This is a powerful declaration of what we as a family will stand for. In Joshua 24:1–15, Joshua spoke to the people on the Lord's behalf. Joshua started by reminding the people that God called Abraham and led him away from all he knew. The verses go on to detail all God did for His people.

In verse 14 we read, "So fear the Lord and serve him wholeheartedly. Put away forever the idols your ancestors worshiped when they lived beyond the Euphrates River and in Egypt. Serve the Lord alone.'" God challenged His people to look at their lives and decide. Would they put away their idols and serve God alone? Joshua boldly declared that his household would serve God alone.

Do you and your household stand for the Lord today? Do you serve Him alone, or do some idols stand in the way?

Pack Your Backpack: Choose One Action Step

1. Choose one day this week to look at each room in the house. Determine if there is any furniture to move around or get rid of to create a more peaceful space.
2. Pick a day to go through each room, one at a time, and see how much clutter you can get rid of.
3. Pick a day to go through each child's bedroom with them, one at a time, and see how much clutter you can get rid of.
4. Choose and implement one of the daily "clear the clutter" ideas. Once you have mastered that habit, choose another.
5. Look at the rooms of your house and find ways to let more sunshine in.
6. Try to make the house quieter. Is the TV on for background noise? Consider choosing a time of day to have no extra noise.

———————

"But if serving the Lord seems undesirable to you, then choose for yourselves this day whom you will serve, whether the gods your ancestors served beyond the Euphrates, or the gods of the Amorites, in whose land you are living. But as for me and my household, we will serve the Lord." (Joshua 24:15)

Please read Joshua 24:15. Before reading, ask the Holy Spirit to reveal something new to you. After reading, please answer the study questions below.

1. Read Joshua 24:1–15. Make a list of all the things God did for His people.

_____

_____

_____

_____

2. Choose one thing from this list that impacted you. Why did it affect you so much?

_____

_____

_____

_____

3. Read Joshua 24:12. When something good has happened, have you ever taken the credit or glory? Confess this to God and ask Him to help you always to give Him the glory.

_____

_____

_____

_____

4. What idols do you have? How will you put them away?

_____

_____

_____

5. What does wholeheartedly serving the Lord look like? What can you do differently in your household serve the Lord with your whole heart?

_____

_____

_____

_____

Gentle Challenge

This chapter is about your home's physical environment. What does your home feel like right now? Ask your spouse or a trusted friend for their thoughts. Write down at least one way you can change the physical environment of your home.

Encouragement

Look through the many ideas for creating an encouraging environment. Start by clearing the large clutter. Plan a time in your calendar to do this. Then move to the day-to-day strategies to create an encouraging environment. Take this one step at a time. Soon your home will feel more encouraging.

Let's Pray

Dear God, thank you for the gift of our home. I long for my home to be a haven for my family. Please help me to create the time to clear our clutter. As I do that, please help me to teach my children the importance of getting rid of clutter. Lord, may you always remain the center of our household. Help us continually to be aware of any idols we need to stop worshipping. We choose to serve you alone, Lord. May our home be a blessing to our family and all who enter. In Jesus' name, amen.

Please write your own prayer here:

_____

_____

_____

_____

Journal

_____

_____

_____

_____

_____

_____

_____

_____

_____

_____

_____

_____

_____

CHAPTER 8
The Emotional Environment of Your Home

By wisdom a house is built, and through understanding it is established; through knowledge its rooms are filled with rare and beautiful treasures.

Proverbs 24:3–4 (NIV)

Now that we have addressed the physical aspect of the home, let's look at ways we can create an encouraging environment in our homes. We will look at ways to cultivate joy, be intentional with the words we speak, model healthy relationships, and help our kids to learn where their identity lies. This chapter will also focus on ways to be present in the home with our families.

Cultivate Joy

If our home is filled with anger and frustration, our kids will feel insecure and will act that way. If your home is filled with joy, your kids will grow in confidence and bring joy wherever they go. What does it mean to cultivate joy in your home?

Joy starts with you. When your children see a joyful attitude in you no matter what comes your way, they will learn to adopt this attitude. Joy comes from deep within and, more importantly, from knowing Jesus as our Lord and Savior. When your kids have a relationship with Jesus, they can have joy, no matter what. I need to be reminded of this. It's important to talk about joy with your kids.

We can also cultivate joy in our homes by laughing together, making time for playing together, and spending time outside. Refer to chapter 6 about enjoying your kids.

Another way to cultivate joy in your home is by practicing gratitude. When we are grateful for all we have, joy will overflow in our lives. Take time each day to share what you are grateful for. Encourage your kids to keep a gratitude journal.

Another way to cultivate joy in our homes is to refuse to kill the joy. Sometimes things happen, and we feel angry or upset with one another. We may complain, whine, or mumble things under our breath when we are upset. These are natural human reactions, but that doesn't mean they're okay. In our home, we often remind our kids of Philippians 2:14: "Do everything without complaining and arguing." When they say or write this Scripture verse, it reminds them how God wants us to live.

We need to teach our kids and ourselves how to keep from killing the joy in our homes. First, we must learn to ask ourselves the root of our emotion. Then write it out or tell someone. Depending on the age of your kids, you might need to help them.

Another strategy is to wear a bracelet or rubber band on your wrist. Every time you grumble or complain, you have to move the bracelet to the other wrist. This helps you become more aware of joy killing. The goal is to keep the bracelet on the same wrist for at least twenty-one days.

A third strategy to help you and your children not to kill joy is to look at the big picture. Will the thing you're complaining about matter in five minutes or five days? If not, let it go. If so, move to the fourth strategy: sharing your concern with a trusted friend or mentor. Talking it out can help you get to the root of the complaint. After talking it through, you may conclude you need to address the person who offended you. Guide your kids through this process if necessary. As parents, we can help our kids by letting them share what is bothering them. This is a great way to help them process their emotions and learn to manage them.

The fifth strategy to avoid killing joy in your home is to find the positives in the situation. Challenge yourself and your kids to list at least five positives at that moment. You can talk them out or even list them. That way, you'll see the good in any situation.

Use Words of Encouragement and Praise

Another way to create an encouraging home environment is to use words of encouragement and praise. It sounds easy, but I'm sometimes surprised at my automatic responses. For example, let's say Caleb showed me a picture he drew. If I respond with a hearty "Good job!" it sounds nice and all, but what does it tell him? Does it encourage creativity in him? Am I being specific, telling him exactly what he did well? It's easy to slap a "Good job!" onto anything our kids do or share with us.

Instead, I could have said to Caleb, "I love how you used that light green color for the trees" or "That football field looks like it would be fun to play on." Do you see the difference? I stopped and noticed what Caleb drew and encouraged him with specific praise.

In addition to catching our kids doing something bad, let's catch them doing something good. One Saturday morning, Analiah made an egg sandwich for her daddy for breakfast—all on her own. It was so thoughtful and sweet.

Analiah also made a big mess in the kitchen while making the breakfast. It would have been easy to focus on the mess. Instead, I used it as time to encourage her with words of praise. "It was kind of you to make breakfast for your daddy. Thanks for thinking of him." Afterward, I helped her clean up as a way to show appreciation for what she did for her father.

Let's be on the lookout for ways to praise and encourage our kids. Let this be the normal. As we do, we teach our kids how to treat others, and we set them up for success in their relationships.

Modeling Healthy Relationships

Our kids constantly watch us and take cues from us. When they see us interact with one another, is it loving and kind? Are you patient and respectful to your spouse? Or do you lose your temper easily? How do you treat your extended family? It's important to model healthy relationships.

I understand not all extended-family relationships are healthy. But the way we treat them or talk about them can be healthy. This way, we teach our kids how to love and respect others, even when they are unkind to us.

Sometimes, even though we model healthy relationships, our kids may not follow our example. Especially with their own siblings. When we notice this, we need to address it immediately. Jonathan and I turn to the Bible and show our kids what God says about our treatment of others. Our kids will lose privileges if they continue in the behavior. We look for a heart change in them before they gain their freedoms back. We ask them to spend time in prayer and God's Word. We often ask them to write some Scriptures that focus on how to treat others. Here are a few of the Scriptures we have had them write out and memorize:

> Instead, be kind to each other, tenderhearted, forgiving one another, just as God through Christ has forgiven you. (Ephesians 4:2)

> Since God chose you to be the holy people he loves, you must clothe yourselves with tenderhearted mercy, kindness, humility, gentleness, and patience. (Colossians 3:12)

> The tongue can bring death or life; those who love to talk will reap the consequences. (Proverbs 18:21)

Modeling with Our Words

Our words carry a lot of weight—probably more than we realize. They play a big part in our home's environment. So we must choose wisely. Pause right now and think through the last words you said to your child. Where they positive words or negative? Did the words build up or tear down your child?

This is hard for me to swallow too. Too many times, my words did not build up my children. And not just my words, but also the tone of my voice. Yikes! It's so easy to get frustrated or annoyed when your kid does something they shouldn't have. But our response is what they will hear in their head anytime they mess up. They will start believing our words and tone as truth about who they are.

As a child, I felt I wasn't good enough. I didn't feel loved and accepted. Once I accidently dropped a glass peanut butter jar, and it broke. I sliced my finger on the glass. Blood dripped down my hand. Instead of caring for me, my grandma yelled at me for dropping the peanut butter and told me to clean it up. In the moment, Grandma communicated that the mess was more important than I was.

Do we want to communicate that to our kids? If not, we need to be the voice of encouragement, praise, and patience. But how do we do this if we grew up in a critical home or even a home that didn't know Jesus? As I mentioned before, I didn't grow up in a church that taught us to have a personal relationship with Jesus. I honestly thought I had to earn my way to heaven. But nothing we do can save us. If we don't have a personal relationship with Jesus, it will affect the words we speak. We can't merely stop being a certain way. We must have a heart change. It has to be Jesus.

If you don't have a personal relationship with Jesus, I will walk you through the process of being saved and gaining that relationship.

First, here's some background about Jesus. He came into the world as a baby so we could have life. He went to the cross and took all our sin upon Him (Isaiah 53:5). God the Father even turned away from Him as He died on the cross (Matthew 27:45–46). Jesus's death would mean nothing without the resurrection. After three days, Jesus rose again. He conquered death once and for all. And because He conquered death, we can have eternal life.

How do we get saved? How do we know without a shadow of a doubt where we will spend eternity? Romans 3:23 tells us that "everyone has sinned; we all fall short of God's glorious standard." Therefore, to be saved, we must first agree with God that we are sinners. Because of this sin, we are separated from God. According to Romans 6:23, the penalty for our sin is death. We deserve death, "but God showed his great love for us by sending Christ to die for us while we were still sinners" (Romans 5:8).

The next step is to confess our sin and ask Jesus to be the Lord of our lives. When we do this, we will be saved. "Everyone who calls on the name of the LORD will be saved" (Romans 10:13). We also read in

Romans 10:9–10, "If you openly declare that Jesus is LORD and believe in your heart that God raised him from the dead, you will be saved. For it is by believing in your heart that you are made right with God, and it is by openly declaring your faith that you are saved."

Here is a prayer to pray to receive Jesus as your Lord and Savior:

Dear Jesus, thank you for taking all my sin upon yourself. I confess to you all the ways I have sinned. Please forgive me. I accept your free gift of salvation. Thank you for dying and rising again so I may have eternal life. Please help me to live for you every day of my life. In Jesus' name, amen.

Once you have prayed this prayer, your life will forever change. However, as we walk out this life, we will still struggle and sometimes even sin. That is why it's important to grow continually in our walk with God. Dig into the Bible daily. Read it and apply it to your life. Get involved in a church body that has sound biblical doctrine. This will help you grow closer to God and know Him more.

Find an accountability partner. As you continue to grow and change, this person can support you. They can also challenge you in areas that don't line up with God's Word. Memorize God's Word in areas you struggle with. For example, if, like my grandma, it's hard for you to show love, memorize verses about love:

Since God chose you to be the holy people he loves, you must clothe yourselves with tenderhearted mercy, kindness, humility, gentleness, and patience. (Colossians 3:12)

Love is patient and kind. Love is not jealous or boastful or proud or rude. It does not demand its own way. It is not irritable, and it keeps no record of being wronged. It does not rejoice about injustice but rejoices whenever the truth wins out. Love never gives up, never loses faith, is always hopeful, and endures through every circumstance. (1 Corinthians 13:4–7)

It all comes back to Jesus. He is the only one who can bring heart change in us. We need to surrender our hearts and lives to him continually. We also have the privilege of teaching our children how to do this daily.

As parents, we have the awesome responsibility of instilling in our children the truth of who they are in Christ. We are the ones who pour this into them. If they don't hear it from us, our children will turn to others and not necessarily hear the truth.

Speak Truth

Every day, we need to remind our children who they are in Christ. Why? Because our children need to have the truth rooted in their hearts and minds. They need to believe their identity is found only in God and not in this world. When your children believe the truth, they walk in confidence. Therefore, the best way to build confidence in our kids is to remind them of the truth of who they are in God.

To share the truth with our kids, we must take time each day to reflect on God's Word. Read the Bible together and study the verses that tell us who we are in Christ. Teach your children how to walk that out in their upcoming day.

Another way to share truth with our kids is to post truth around the house. In our kids' bathroom, a sign says, "Hello. Good morning. You're doing great. I believe in you." I don't know about you, but that pours courage into me. It makes me want to tackle the day with excitement. We also have a sign that says, "Always remember you are braver than you know, stronger than you seem, smarter than you think, and loved more than you know." This saying is another powerful truth that pours courage into our kids. It reminds them who they are in Christ.

We've also hung Scripture verse signs around our house. If you don't have signs, you could print Scripture verses on paper and hang them up. Here are a few of my favorite verses.

> "Be strong and courageous. Do not be afraid or terrified because of them, for the LORD your God goes with you; he will never leave you nor forsake you." (Deuteronomy 31:6)

This Scripture verse reminds our kids that they are not alone. God is always with them. No matter what they face, they can be strong and courageous because God is on their side. He will never leave nor forsake our kids.

But those who trust in the LORD will find new strength. They
will soar high on wings like eagles. They will run and not grow
weary. They will walk and not faint. (Isaiah 40:31)

For the moments when your kids feel weary, make sure you've planted
this Scripture in their minds. God will help your kids soar on wings like
eagles. He will help them run in life and not grow weary. The key is trust-
ing in the Lord. We need to encourage our kids to choose to turn to God
for new strength.

And I am certain that God, who began the good work within
you, will continue his work until it is finally finished on the day
when Christ Jesus returns. (Philippians 1:6)

God is working in our children's lives. We need to remind them
of this. In the moments when they doubt that and their situation feels
hopeless, remind them to reflect on this Scripture verse. God is using every
situation in our children's lives to draw them closer to Himself. He is
working out everything for their good.

"Don't be afraid, for I am with you. Don't be discouraged, for
I am your God. I will strengthen you and help you. I will hold
you up with my victorious right hand." (Isaiah 41:10)

Our kids will have fear and worry about many things. We must
remind them that God wants to help them. He wants to strengthen and
help our children. God also wants to remind them that they are not alone.
Encourage them to take a deep breath and rest in the arms of their heavenly
Daddy. Remind your children that God will not let them fall.

So, let's not get tired of doing what is good. At just the right
time we will reap a harvest of blessing if we don't give up.
(Galatians 6:9)

Often our kids feel tired and weary. They may even feel as if nothing
they do matters. Encourage them with this Scripture verse. Remind them
to tap into the Holy Spirit. Encourage them to ask God for wisdom and

strength. Remind them that He is on their side, and because of that, they can keep going and not give up.

Another way to help our kids speak truth is by writing affirmations (truth statements) about who they are in Christ. Each day, have your child read them out loud. As they do this, truth will sink in. When your child doubts their worth, these affirmations can pull them back to God's truth.

We can use the truth statements in many ways. We can have a list, index cards, or printed cards available for the child to read each day. We can create a recording of the truth statements for our children to listen to. One more way to use truth statements is to write a few in a notebook each day. Writing something out is a great way to remember the truth. Choose whichever way will help your kids hide God's truth in their hearts.

Some examples of truth statements are:

- I am fearfully and wonderfully made (Psalm 139:13).
- I am chosen and dearly loved (Colossians 3:12).
- I am a child of God (John 1:12).
- I am accepted in Christ (Romans 15:7).
- I am God's masterpiece (Ephesians 2:10).
- I am created in God's image (Genesis 1:27).
- I am a new creation in Christ (2 Corinthians 5:17).
- I am forgiven and free in Christ (Acts 13:38–39).
- I am blessed because of Christ (Ephesians 1:3).
- I am made complete in Christ (Colossians 2:10).

Speak Life-Giving Words

Life-giving words build us up instead of tearing us down. They bring life as we pour courage into someone. We need to speak these words constantly to our children and to ourselves.

I recently gained some weight. I beat myself up about it because I was discouraged and felt fat. I had to be careful how I spoke about my weight around our children, especially our girls. Even though I felt fat, I didn't call myself fat. I didn't want to teach our kids that it was okay to talk to themselves that way.

Unfortunately, we hear negative words everywhere we turn. Our children hear negative words at school and even at the grocery store. Words like dumb, stupid, ugly, jerk, annoying, fat, etc. Do not allow these words in your home, even though they hear them in other places.

I encourage you to make a list of life-giving words your children can speak in the home and even outside the home. That way, when you or your children speak a negative word (because unfortunately, it does happen), you can reference this list and think of other words to speak to one another instead.

Our homes need to be safe havens for our children. This means we don't allow negative talk toward themselves or anyone else in the home. One way we have helped with this is by monitoring the music, movies, and shows our kids watch.

Analiah and Caleb wanted to watch a show on Disney Plus. It looked cute and innocent. Both my husband and I watched it with them at separate times. It was a fun show, but one kid in the show spoke disrespectfully to his dad and grandma. The grandma bullied other people and was manipulative with her old-lady status so she could get what she wanted. It was subtle and made to be funny. But we are not okay with our younger kids receiving that input on how to treat others. Jonathan and I talked with them and shared why we don't want them to continue to watch the show. Caleb and Analiah weren't happy about not being able to watch the show anymore, but I know they understood why.

Sometimes we don't have control over what our kids watch. For example, the babysitter or their friend's family might have different standards than you. In this instance, I encourage you to talk with your kids about guarding their hearts and minds when watching movies or shows. Teach them to close their eyes or turn away when a scene doesn't honor God.

Another way to help with this is to discuss the shows at the end of the day. Talk about what they saw and help them work through any fears they may have gained from watching a show. Help them to see God's truth about the show. Try not to react at what they share. Be open and listen so they know you're a safe place to share.

If the shows or movies shown at the babysitter's house become a real problem, talk with the babysitter about your concerns. If the babysitter doesn't care or refuses to make changes, take your kids elsewhere. I understand that finding childcare can be hard. But when we honor God and protect our kids, God will provide another babysitter. Take this concern to God and watch Him answer your prayer with something better than you imagined.

Be Present

As parents, we need to be present with our children in our home. Not just physically but emotionally too. This will make a big difference in our home's emotional environment. So how do you be present as a parent? I'm glad you asked.

First, when your child talks to you, take time to listen. You may be in the middle of something, such as making dinner. If you are able to stop and listen, that is great. But if you need to keep an eye on the pasta, tell your child you would love to give them your full attention, but they need to wait until you can walk away from the noodles.

In chapter 5 we talked about "stop, look, and listen." This is definitely something to pack in your Intentional Backpack. Fully listening can be hard, but it's important because it communicates to your child that they are important enough to be heard.

Another way to be present is to put away your phones. Maybe even literally lock them in a cupboard. I implemented this a couple of years ago. I involved the kids in the process. If they caught me pulling out my phone during family time, I owed them a quarter. You can bet they paid attention. It freed me up to focus on them during our time together. I also learned that life continued on just fine without me checking social media. I encourage you to pick a time during your day when you lock up the phones. Implement this as a family and see how much more present you are.

Another way to be more present with your children is to have daily routines with them. This will show your kids that they are important to you. One morning routine could be asking the children how you can pray for them. We can ask this at the bus stop, in the car on the way to school, or at the breakfast table.

Another idea for a new daily routine is sharing highs and lows at the end of the school day. This provides a great time to hear about our kids' school days and to show them that you truly care about their day. When my kids and I do this after school, I also share my highs and lows. That way, they get a glimpse into my world too. Sharing your lows could possibly cause anxiety in your children, so be cautious with what and how you share. But also, be real. Our kids need to see that you struggle too. It shows them how to respond to lows in their lives, and it can point them toward Jesus in their lows.

Bedtime Routine

Bedtimes can be a great time to connect with your kids. It can also give an opportunity for one-on-one time. Take at least ten or fifteen minutes with each child. Ask your kids about their day. If they don't have much to tell you, tell them about your day and what you were grateful for.

Then ask your kids some questions, such as "What do you look forward to tomorrow?" or "What are you worried about?" Wrap up this connection time by praying for your child. This would also be a good time to review the Bible verse your kids are memorizing or read a Bible story together.

Depending on the number of kids and the amount of time you have, you may be able to do this each day. Or you can pick a certain day for each child. Do whatever works best for your family.

Showing Affection

Showing affection can change the emotional environment of your home in powerful ways. Your children need lots of hugs every day. Fill their love tank with physical touch. Remember chapter 6, where we talked about kids needing at least two or three hugs each day? Make sure you hug your kids.

They also need to see you and your spouse showing affection. Yes, your children may yell "Gross! Stop kissing!" But inside, they like it. It helps your child to feel more secure. When you and your spouse show affection, your kids see healthy ways to relate to their future spouse.

Spend Time with Your Kids

As we discussed in chapter 6, one-on-one time with your children is important. The emotional environment of your home will be healthy when you take time to be with your children. Here are a few more ideas for spending time with your kids around the home.

Clean Out the Garage

The garage is one place that will always need some cleaning up, so ask one of your children to help. Give them simple or hard jobs to do, depending on their age. This is a great way to clear the clutter while spending time with your kids.

Bubble Fight

There are always dishes to wash, right? Sometimes that can be frustrating. Why not make it a fun time with your kids? Fill the sink with dishwater and extra soap to create lots of bubbles. Invite one of your children to wash dishes with you. They can either wash, rinse, or just dry the dishes, depending on their age. End the time with a bubble fight.

Go Down Memory Lane

Pull out old photo albums or scrapbooks, sit down with your kids, and take a stroll down memory lane. If you have baby books or pictures of your child's birth, talk about what you felt when you saw them for the first time.

Look through your other photo albums or pictures on the computer or your phone, and reminisce. If you have a wedding album or even just pictures, pull that out to show your kids. Tell them the story of how you fell in love with their dad.

Another option for going down memory lane is to look at photo albums filled with pictures from vacations, birthdays, and holidays you spent together over the years. It's also fun to share stories of your adventures as a child. Kids love to hear stories of when you were their age.

Cook or Bake with Your Child

Pick a recipe to cook or bake with your child. Choose a recipe you loved as a kid, or use a tried and true one. You could also try a new recipe together. Cooking or baking together is a great way to be present with your children and get to know them.

Be aware of the emotional environment of your home. Children will often act out when they need attention. If you notice your child doing this, take a look at your home's environment. What does it lack right now? Have you spent time with them recently? Has the schedule gotten so full that you've neglected your daily habit of connecting with your kids? What is the status on words in your home? Are they life giving?

We can do a lot to create an encouraging environment in our homes. I encourage you to add the things we discussed to your Intentional Backpack. Work on one idea at a time until you master it. Then add another idea to your backpack when you feel ready. Let's work toward a healthy environment in our homes.

By wisdom a house is built, and through understanding it is established; through knowledge its rooms are filled with rare and beautiful treasures. (Proverbs 24:3–4)

Often, when we think about building a home, we think of materials like steel, wood, concrete, stone, or brick. These are all important for building a home. In Proverbs 24:3–4, Solomon goes a little deeper than the physical materials used to build a home—he refers to our spiritual and moral home. We need God's wisdom if we want to build our home. Only through God's wisdom can understanding be established. We must keep God at the center of our homes.

God floods us with His wisdom, knowledge, and understanding. I don't know about you, but I'd rather depend on God's wisdom, knowledge, and understanding than my own futile efforts. As we depend on God, the rooms of our house will be filled with rare and beautiful treasures.

Then His wisdom and understanding will guide and strengthen us in all situations. God loves to supply all our needs. We serve an amazing God.

Pack Your Backpack: Choose One Action Step

- Choose one way to cultivate joy mentioned in this chapter and implement it in your home.
- When your child brings a paper or drawing to show you, pause and listen. Use specific words of encouragement and praise in your response. Notice how your child reacts.
- Implement identity statements with your kids. Together, make a list based on God's truth.
- Take note of the shows or movies your kids watch. Do these programs use life-giving words, or are they filled with negative words?
- Choose one of the ways to be more present with your child. Share it with your spouse or a friend, and ask them to hold you accountable.
- Choose one of the activities you and your child can do to be more present in the home. What is one thing you discovered about your child from that time?

By wisdom a house is built, and through understanding it is established; through knowledge its rooms are filled with rare and beautiful treasures. (Proverbs 24:3–4)

Ask the Holy Spirit to reveal something new to you from Proverbs 24:3–4. Then answer the study questions below.

1. How is a house built?

_____

_____

_____

_____

2. How is a house established?

_____

_____

_____

3. What rare and beautiful treasures fill your house? Hint: It is not just physical things.

_____

_____

_____

4. What do you need wisdom for right now? Pause now and ask God for wisdom. Sit in His presence and journal about what He is saying to you.

_____

_____

_____

5. Read Matthew 7:24–29. How do these verses relate to Proverbs 24:3–4? What did God teach you through Matthew 7:24–29?

_____

_____

_____

Gentle Challenge

Your home's emotional environment is just as important as the physical. I daresay it is more important. Take time this week to evaluate your home's emotional environment. Think about what needs to change. When you've implemented one of the ideas listed above, notice the change it brings.

Encouragement

Your home's physical environment may not look as you want it to right now. Be encouraged that God will help you change this. Read back through the section about cultivating joy in your home. Start with this and continue from there. The physical environment of your home will not change overnight. Be patient and lean into God's wisdom and strength for this.

Let's Pray

Dear God, thank you once again for our home. Lord, I want it to be an emotionally healthy place for our children. Please help me to cultivate joy and model it to our children every day. Teach me self-control with my words. Help me to speak words of life in our home. Thank you, Holy Spirit, for your guidance and wisdom in this. In Jesus' name, amen.

Please write your own prayer here:

_____

_____

_____

_____

Journal

_____

_____

_____

_____

_____

_____

_____

_____

_____

_____

_____

_____

_____

_____

PART FIVE

Life Beyond the Home: Strong Identity Leads to Releasing World Changers

CHAPTER 9
On Mission

———◆———

*Therefore, go and make disciples of all nations, baptizing them
in the name of the Father and of the Son and of the Holy Spirit.*
Matthew 28:19

The journey to becoming an intentional family is not meant for us alone. We become an intentional family so we can be on mission to reflect God and bless everyone we come in contact with. This chapter will focus on developing a mission statement and creating family goals. It will also discuss the importance of a family calendar and finding ways to serve others.

When you hear the words "on mission," what do you think of? Maybe the movie *Mission: Impossible* or going on a mission trip. The mission we're talking about is possible and could even involve a mission trip.

To be on mission means to be focused, intent, and moving forward. In our case, it's being focused on God and the mission He gave us before he left earth. The mission is found in Matthew 28:19: "Therefore, go and make disciples of all the nations, baptizing them in the name of the Father and the Son and the Holy Spirit." One of the most important responsibilities of a parent is helping our kids be on mission for God.

Family Mission Statement
One way Jonathan and I have made this a priority is by creating a mission statement for our family. A mission statement increases your effectiveness

as a family. This mission statement helps families come together and have a goal in mind. We can use it as a reference when making decisions. How do we create a family mission statement? Let's talk through some simple steps.

First, plan a family meeting. Bake a favorite dessert or pick up a treat from the store. Maybe even get some balloons to hang around the room or on the kids' chairs. Set the mood by creating a positive environment. Make this a fun time together.

Start the family meeting with prayer. Ask God to guide you in writing your family mission statement, and make sure it's rooted in God's Word. Pray Psalm 127:1 over your time together: "Unless the LORD builds a house, the work of the builders is wasted."

Next, explain what a mission statement is and the importance of having one. Tell your kids that your family is going to create a mission statement. Remind them that everyone's input is valuable and needed.

Our Home

First, talk about your home. Ask your children how they want your home to feel. What makes them want to come home? Write down their answers so you can reference them when you create your mission statement. Ask each family member how they want others to feel when they come to your house. Take time to listen to everyone. You may be surprised at some of your kids' answers.

Our Family

Next, ask your children what kind of family they want to be. Discuss the ways your family wants to speak and act with each other. What does each family member want to be known for? Ask your children how your family can help others learn about Jesus. Take time to listen to one another. Talk about ways to serve others in your community.

Our Values

Last, discover what values are important to your family. Create a list with everyone's answers. The list may include forgiveness, creativity, adventure, faith, honesty, and hospitality. Be sure to list everyone's ideas and listen well. I encourage you to make sure your values are based on God's Word.

Creating the Mission Statement

Great job going through those questions together! Now, you get to have fun creating the mission statement. When you look at all the responses, you'll probably find similar ideas. Group these together and make everyone's ideas part of the mission statement. When the kids realize you've used their ideas, they'll own the mission statement.

The mission statement will guide your family interactions with one another and others. It can consist of a single sentence, three or four bullet points, or a paragraph. Since your family values are based on God's Word, use the Scriptures to guide your mission statement. Feel free to use a specific Scripture verse as a guide.

For example, let's say you choose Colossians 3:12: "Since God chose you to be the holy people he loves, you must clothe yourselves with tenderhearted mercy, kindness, humility, gentleness, and patience." Based on this verse, your family mission statement could read: "Our family is humble and thinks of others before ourselves. We are kind and patient with one another."

Here is another example:

In Our Family:
We speak with gentleness and kindness (Proverbs 15:1).
We obey with joyful hearts (Colossians 3:20).
We show love and respect for others (1 Peter 2:17).
We love the Lord our God with all our hearts (Deuteronomy 6:5).

How to Use Your Family Mission Statement

Once you have completed your family mission statement, start using it. Type it up and hang it where the whole family can see it. Or make several copies to hang around the house. Another option is to make a printable of it to frame and hang on the wall or on top of a bookshelf. Find someone who can make it into a wooden sign, or have a custom print made on Etsy.

Another fun idea is to make it into a song to help your family memorize it. Do whatever works best for your family.

Read your mission statement daily or every other day. As a family, work on memorizing the mission statement. This will help you live it out. When your kids get into a fight, reference your mission statement. Are they being kind and patient? Use it as a guide to bring change in your home.

Each time your family needs to make a decision, reference your mission statement. Does it line up with who your family is? If so, you have your answer. If not, you can be confident with your no. You'll be asked to do many things that will fill the calendar. Instead of letting things dictate your schedule, let your family mission statement help you make decisions.

The mission statement may change over time as your family does. You may add a new family member. Your children will also grow, so feel free to revisit your family mission statement every five years or more as needed.

If Your Husband Isn't On Board

Some husbands will not get behind this idea. If this is the case in your home, try to understand his reasons. First, realize this may not be a passion of his. He simply may not care about having a mission statement. I encourage you to talk to your husband candidly about this. If he doesn't want one, that is okay, but you could ask him to consider supporting your desire to have one.

Your husband may truly not understand why having a mission statement is important. You have spent time reading and learning about it, and if you work outside the home, you've spent your precious few free minutes studying the concept. However, your husband has not. So instead of bombarding him with facts about mission statements and how great they are, break it down into small chunks to explain it. Take your time. Approach it in a way that shares what you have been thinking instead of merely telling him, "We need to do this because . . ." Answer all your husband's questions.

If your husband doesn't want to have a mission statement, then you need to trust him. Remember how we talked about being under the umbrella of our husband's leadership? We don't want to step outside it. If having a mission statement is truly a desire of your heart, then pray about it. Your husband may eventually come around. Either way, you need to trust God's plan for your husband's authority in the home.

Anchored Family Guide

Another way to be on mission as family is to take time to create goals for the new year. In November or December, our family plans a time to reflect on the past year. We go out to dinner to celebrate the year. Each family member shares their favorite memories, and we talk about the hard times too. It is a great time to reflect and see God's hand over the year.

After that celebration, we use the Anchored Family Guide to plan our next year. The Anchored Family Guide is a resource Jonathan and I have created for families. It comes in a downloadable version. You can order it from my website. In the paragraphs that follow, I'll share a little more about this resource.

Before coming to the planning time, we have taken time to look in and look back, using the worksheets the Anchored Family Guide provides. We look at ways we have personally grown and ways we want to be different in the upcoming year. The looking-back questions help us to reflect on the things we accomplished as a family and the ways God has helped our family change for the good.

During Anchored Family time, we look at each member's strengths and talk about ways we can use those strengths to serve others. Together, we pick ways to serve during the coming year.

Then we talk through the things we would like to do as a family over the next year. It's fun to hear everyone's responses. The ideas are silly, fun, and serious. They become our goals for the year.

We also talk through habits that would help us to be successful in the coming year. We decide on four habits to develop as a family. Last, we brainstorm a Crazy Big Dream for the year. This is something that seems impossible but fits our family's passions and desires. (Be sure to reference your family mission statement for this part.) I love this time to connect as a family and get ready for the coming year.

Word of the Year

Another way to be on mission as a family is to have a family word of the year. This word can give us a growth focus. The word is meant to represent a central way your family will depend on God in the year to come. It helps you determine who you want to become as a family. This word helps your family to be intentional about how you spend your hours, days, and months.

We use the Family Word of the Year Printable found at https://anastasiacorbin.com/word-of-the-year/. We worked through the reflection questions provided. I love this time to reflect as a family. We asked God to show us what He wanted to grow in our family this year. All our children were involved in this process.

Our word of the year is "joy." As a family, it has been so fun to look for ways to choose joy. It is amazing to me how much God has used it to change us.

Family Calendar

Another way to be on mission is to have a family calendar. That way, you can see what you are committed to and maybe even what you can let go of. Remember, we want to simplify and let go of things that don't bring life or help us to be more attentive to one another. But how do we keep track of what we have going on each week? Why do we need a family calendar?

The family calendar can become an anchor point for your children. It helps them to know and feel more secure about what is going on. If your kids are anything like ours, they love to know what will happen each day or what they have to look forward to that week. Our kids can see this information in two different areas.

We have a magnetic calendar on our refrigerator. It is a schedule of the week. The dinners for each evening are listed but are subject to change. This board includes appointments, evening activities, kids' sports practices, our date night, and church activities. If Jonathan or I have an accountability meeting with a mentor or an outing with a friend, it goes on the board. It also has a section for what is coming up in the following week. The kids love referencing this board. It answers a lot of their questions.

We also have a paper calendar that lists all the activities of the month and even some things later in the year. It's easy for me to forget to add things to this calendar, since I store everything on my phone, but my kids don't see that. So I'm trying to make a priority of keeping this calendar current.

When an activity comes up, we consult the family calendar. Do we have the capacity to take on this activity? If it's a longer commitment, such as a sport, can we sustain the schedule? Would it be too much on the family? When our kids were younger, we didn't have as many activities because it took a lot of time and energy to raise four young children, and we didn't have much energy to give. We were cautious in saying yes to anything.

Now it still takes a lot of time and energy to raise our four children, but we have more energy to take on different activities. Again, we reference the big picture before we add anything to our family calendar. How about you? Do you have a family calendar? Do you have a place where your children can see the bigger picture? When you know the family calendar, you can be on mission as a family and take on opportunities to serve.

On Mission in Your Hometown and around the World

We can all find many ways to serve as a family in our hometowns. Is there a soup kitchen in your area? Pick a time to serve as a family. Is there a food pantry? Ask them for a list of their greatest needs. On a family fun night, shop for these items and take them to the food pantry. If you can, help to stock shelves or do whatever else the pantry needs.

Another way to serve your community is to make blessing bags for the homeless. How often do you see someone stationed at a traffic light or in a plaza parking lot, asking for money? A blessing bag is a great way to give these people the things they may need.

Here is a list of supplies for food blessing bags:

- Gallon-size zippered bags to put the items in
- Water bottles
- Crackers
- Granola bars

- Peanuts or nuts of any kind
- Dried fruit
- Trail mix
- Gum
- Canned tuna or chicken salad
- Fruit cup or applesauce (include a spoon)

Here is a list of supplies for toiletries/winter blessing bags:

- Gallon-size zippered bags
- Toothbrush
- Toothpaste
- Floss
- Soap
- Deodorant
- Shampoo and conditioner
- Comb
- Sunscreen
- Chapstick
- Small bandages
- Baby wipes
- Hand sanitizer
- Washcloth
- Socks
- Gloves
- Hats
- Hand warmers

Once you have gathered all the supplies, put the bags together as a family. After they are all packed, lay hands on the bags. Ask each family member to pray and ask God to use these bags to encourage the people you give them to. Then store these bags in the trunk of your car until you see a need.

Praying for the Homeless

Now that we have bags stored in the back of our vehicles, we're ready to give them away. This is a great opportunity to teach your kids to pray for someone in need. We ask the person how we can pray for them. It began with just Jonathan or me praying for the homeless person. Now, when we see someone, we send the older kids to take them the bag. They initiate praying for them. It is so awesome to see how they love people in their time of need. I love hearing what they prayed for when they get back to the vehicle. This is what being on mission for Jesus is about.

Mission Trips

Mission trips are a great way to be on mission as a family. Does your church offer opportunities to take mission trips? If not, I encourage you to check out any neighboring churches to see what they have to offer.

If your family is not at the stage to go on a mission trip, I encourage you or your spouse to go alone. This will model to your kids the importance of mission trips. Our church sponsors an orphanage in Cambodia and one in Thailand. In 2011, I went on a mission trip to visit these homes. This experience changed my life. I loved sharing about it with our kids when I got back.

In fact, I loved the Asia's Hope mission trip so much that I went back two more times. Jonathan also went once. We are teaching our kids that mission trips are important. One of our goals is to take a trip with Asia's Hope when our youngest has reached the age of twelve.

You don't have to go far to go on a mission trip. During college, I went to Kentucky to serve people in Harlan County. It was an eye-opening experience for me and taught me a lot about being grateful for what I have. I also learned a lot about hard work and how much it changes you from the inside out. Do some research and find a mission trip that could work for your family.

The journey to becoming an intentional family is not meant for us alone. We are made to be on mission to reflect God and share His redeeming love with others. One way to be on mission is to create a family mission statement. This statement is meant to tell others what your family is about and to guide your decisions. It keeps you grounded and helps your children to feel secure, being a part of something bigger.

Part of being on mission is having a clear vision for your year. What is most important to you? What will fill up your family calendar? What word represents how you want to grow as a family this year? Other ways to be on mission are caring for the homeless in your community or going on a mission trip. Choose any of the ideas that resonate with you from this chapter to help your family be on mission. What will you add to your Intentional Backpack today?

———————

Then Jesus came to them and said, "All authority in heaven and on earth has been given to me. Therefore, go and make disciples of all nations, baptizing them in the name of the Father and of the Son and of the Holy Spirit, and teaching them to obey everything I have commanded you. And surely, I am with you always, to the very end of the age." (Matthew 28:18–20)

In most Bibles, the subtitle of these verses is "The Great Commission." The disciples were at the mountain where Jesus told them to go. He came to them and spoke these powerful words.

Jesus began the Great Commission by reminding them that all authority in heaven and on earth had been given to Him. Jesus's authority is the basis for this mission. This is not a mission we can do in our own strength.

Jesus speaks the same words to us. He asks us to go and make disciples of all the nations. As followers of Jesus, our life mission is to tell others about Him. We don't have to do this on our own. We have the Holy Spirit to guide us. God will bring people into our lives so we can share the gospel with them. Let's be open and aware of how He is working and encourage our kids to do the same.

Pack Your Backpack: Choose One Action Step

1. Plan a time to create a family mission statement. Consider serving a special dessert or putting up decorations to make this a fun time.

2. Display your family mission statement around the house, using one of the ideas listed. Reference it daily.

3. Use the Anchored Family Guide found in my online store to anchor your family for this upcoming year.

4. Spend time going through the family word of the year exercise together. Make it a fun time to connect by going to a special place.

5. Find a calendar that will work well for your family. Post it in an easily accessible spot for your kids.

6. Research mission trips to take as a family. If your children are too young, consider going on a mission trip by yourself.

> Then Jesus came to them and said, "All authority in heaven and on earth has been given to me. Therefore, go and make disciples of all nations, baptizing them in the name of the Father and of the Son and of the Holy Spirit, and teaching them to obey everything I have commanded you. And surely, I am with you always, to the very end of the age." (Matthew 28:18–20)

Please read Matthew 28:18–20. Before reading, ask the Holy Spirit to reveal something new to you. After reading, please answer the study questions below.

1. What mission did Jesus give us in these verses?

_____

_____

_____

_____

2. What is your response to that mission? Is it guilt, apathy, or excitement? Something else?

_____

_____

_____

_____

3. What keeps you from talking about Jesus to your family, friends, or strangers?

_____

_____

_____

_____

4. When was the last time you invited someone to church? Who can you invite this week?

_____

_____

_____

_____

5. How do you lead your family in the mission Jesus gave us?

_____

_____

_____

_____

Gentle Challenge

The journey to becoming an intentional family is not meant for us alone. We become an intentional family so we can be on mission to reflect God and bless all we come in contact with. Take note of how you are doing this as a family. What needs to change?

Encouragement

Being on mission as a family may seem overwhelming, depending on the stage of life your family is in. Take time to talk about this with your spouse or a trusted friend. Read through the section on creating a family mission statement, and start there. Once you have that established, review the other ideas and decide what you want to implement in your family.

Let's Pray

Dear God, thank you for calling our family to be on mission. Lord, please guide us in what that means for us in this season of life and how we can be on mission as a family. Please help us to reflect you in all we say and do. May people see you in us and want more of you, Lord. In Jesus' name, amen.

Please write your own prayer here:

_____

_____

_____

_____

Journal

_____

_____

_____

_____

_____

_____

_____

_____

_____

_____

_____

_____

_____

_____

_____

_____

_____

_____

_____

_____

CHAPTER 10
Conclusion: A Resource for the Intentional Family

———✦———

Have I not commanded you? Be strong and courageous. Do not be afraid; do not be discouraged, for the Lord your God will be with you wherever you go.
Joshua 1:9

Have you ever gone to a conference and walked away completely fired up? You had so many new ideas that you couldn't wait to get home and try them all. Then, did you feel so overwhelmed with the changes that you quit?

I have been there and done that more times that I can count. This book is filled with lots of ideas for becoming an intentional family. You might try some of them but not others. That's okay. This book is intended as a resource for you to come back to often. A book that has sticky notes or dog-eared pages. A book that is your friend in this amazing journey of parenting.

As I mentioned at the beginning of the book, our parenting plays a big part in helping our children know they belong. But parenting is not the only piece. Throughout this book, I've shared how your marriage relationship, the time you spend together as a family, and the environment of your home are all part of the bigger picture. We cannot become an intentional family without each piece. Let's do a quick review of each aspect of becoming an intentional family and why it is important.

Family

We looked at several ways to come together as a family. Family fun nights help children know they have place to belong. It also helps family members learn to laugh together and enjoy each other's company.

Family devotions connect your family to our ultimate source of wisdom: God. As we teach our kids to dig into God's Word, they learn that He will always be with them.

Family vacations are a great way to build family identity. As you experience new places, you get to know one another in different settings. Family dinners are a way to build a stronger family bond. These dinners communicate to our children that they are worth our time.

We also talked about the importance of celebrating as a family. Celebrations bring families together and help create lasting memories. As the family gathers to celebrate and create traditions, members find comfort and security because they have a place to belong. Celebrations are often passed from generation to generation, so children get to know their heritage. When they understand their past and know they belong to something bigger than themselves, confidence is instilled.

Celebrations bring families together and help create meaningful memories. Celebrating helps your children to have a place to belong, and it bonds the family in a special way. As your children move out and start families of their own, they will remember all the ways the family celebrated.

Marriage

Family begins at the wedding. The marriage relationship is the number one priority under our relationship with God. In Matthew 19:5, we read, "And he said, 'This explains why a man leaves his father and mother and is joined to his wife, and the two are united into one.'" This Scripture verse clearly reminds us that when we marry our spouse, we are to leave our family of origin. All too often, we cling to our family because that is what is comfortable and what we know. But we need to make our marriage the priority relationship above our extended family.

The marriage relationship is also above your role as a parent. In the busyness of life, we often forget this truth. Work takes a lot of our time, not to mention all the work around the house.

When the kids are younger, their needs are demanding. As they get older, their needs change, but they still require a lot of time. It can be easy to let kids become the priority in the family. We must not let this happen.

But how do we do this, especially in the culture we live in? Our marriage relationship can be the priority. We talked about the importance of date nights and how to make them work. We also discussed making time for weekend getaways. This is possible even if we don't have family in the area.

The marriage section of the book wrapped up with the five habits of a healthy marriage. Which of the five habits resonated with you? Was it the habit of prayer, Bible reading, couch time, speaking highly of one another, or making sex a priority? Choose one to make a priority until you master it, then work on another habit. One thing I love about marriage is the room to grow. Jonathan and I still work on these habits.

Parenting

In the parenting section, we looked at getting to know our children. We discussed ways to make sure they feel loved and seen. Knowing your child's love language is important. But even more than that is speaking their love language once you know it.

We also talked about using Scripture to pray through areas in our children's lives that they need to grow in. We also discussed using praying hands as a tangible reminder to pray for our kids.

Implementing stop, look, and listen is another way to parent intentionally. It causes us to pay attention to our children and communicate to them that they are worth our time. We also discussed the power of our words. What we say to our children matters. Do our words tear down our kids or build them up?

Another thing we discussed was whether we enjoy our kids. How would they answer that question? Let's be parents who thoroughly enjoy our children, no matter how they act or what they do. We can do this by having one-on-one times with our kids during the week. Monthly outings with Mom or Dad help our children to see we value time with them.

We can enjoy our kids more by taking time to hug them each day and by reading to them, even when they are older. Play is an important part of connecting with your child and learning to enjoy them. Simplifying your family calendar goes a long way in enjoying your kids. You will all have breathing room and feel more peaceful, which helps you all to enjoy each other.

Home

The physical environment of our home plays a big role in creating meaningful memories and building confidence in our kids. When you walk into your home, does it feel inviting? Does it feel like a haven? How do you think it feels to your kids?

We discussed ways to clear the clutter in our homes so it would feel calmer and more peaceful. We also looked at ways to let the sun shine in and how to eliminate the noise that can fill our homes.

We also talked about ways to create an encouraging environment in our homes. We learned how to cultivate joy. The words we speak in our relationships matter. We can find ways to help our kids to learn where their identity lies. The chapter wrapped up with focusing on being present in the home with our families.

Life Beyond the Home

In the "On Mission" chapter, we talked about how the journey to be an intentional family is not meant for us alone. We are made to be on mission to reflect God and share His redeeming love with others. This chapter shared how a family mission statement and setting goals help us in this process.

Below you will find discussion questions for your own personal use or to go over with a group. At the end of those questions, I leave you with a reminder and encouragement.

Discussion Questions for Group or Personal Study

1. Why do you think family fun nights build family identity and help your children feel they belong?
2. What was one of your favorite family vacations as a child and why?
3. Did you sit down for dinner as a family when you were a child? If so, what was the atmosphere? If not, how do you see family dinners as helpful for your family now?
4. Why do you think reading the Bible together as a family is important?
5. Have you ever thought about celebrating answered prayers? Besides the idea given in chapter 2, what are some ways to celebrate answered prayers?
6. When you were a child, what was your favorite way to celebrate your birthday with your family? Do you have this tradition in your family now?
7. What do you think of celebrating salvation birthdays? Is this something you want to do in your family?
8. What are some of your holiday traditions? (Either current traditions or those you observed as a child)
9. Do you think date nights are important? Why or why not?
10. Is the weekend getaway a new concept to you? Do you want to do this in your marriage?
11. Which of the five habits for a stronger marriage stood out to you and why?
12. Do you think couch time is important? Why or why not?
13. Do you think it's important to know your child's love language? Why or why not?

14. What did you think of picking specific Scripture verses to memorize together related to your child's growth point? Do you want to do this in your family?

15. Do you think it's important to have one-on-one time with your child? Why or why not?

16. How can you simplify your family life? What one step can you do today to move toward a simpler life?

17. When your walk into your home, does it feel inviting? Does it feel like a haven? If not, what can you change?

18. How does clutter affect your kids? Why do you think it's important to get rid of the clutter?

19. What does the emotional environment of your home look like right now? What can you do to improve the environment?

20. Do you think daily routines are important for your children? Why or why not?

21. Do you think a family mission statement is important for your family? Why or why not?

22. What are some ways your family has been on mission in your community or around the world?

A Reminder and Encouragement

This book is packed with ideas. It is not meant to overwhelm you but to be a guide on the journey to becoming an intentional family. Choose one idea at a time to implement. Once you have mastered it, come back for more ideas to add to your Intentional Family Backpack. My prayer is that this book can be an encouragement for your family in the years to come.

I leave you with one of my favorite Bible verses.

> "Have I not commanded you? Be strong and courageous. Do not be afraid; do not be discouraged, for the LORD your God will be with you wherever you go." (Joshua 1:9)

This verse begins with a question. If we look back in Joshua 1:6–8, God told Joshua three times that he would need to be strong and courageous in order to defeat the Canaanites, who outnumbered the Israelites. They not only outnumbered them, but the Canaanites were also giants. God wanted to make sure Joshua knew what was required of him.

God wants you to remember that He has given you the same commands. This is not a suggestion for you. It is a command. In this verse, God also reminds us not to be afraid or discouraged. Many things can cause us to fear or feel discouraged. But God is with us wherever we go.

It's incredible to think about the fact that God, the Creator of the universe, is with us. He is right there beside you, filling you up with whatever you need in the journey to building an intentional family. I encourage you to lean into the Lord your God and be strong in Him alone.

It has been an honor to take this journey with you. I know you have what it takes to become an intentional family, because Jesus is in you! Let's continue creating meaningful memories and building confidence in our kids!

Notes

1. Bob and Emilie Barnes, *15 Minute Devotions for Couples* (Oregon: Harvest House, 1995)

2. Jodie Berndt, *Praying the Scriptures for Your Children,* (Michigan: Zondervan Books, 2001)

3. Crystal Bowman and Elena Kucharik, *The One Year Devotions for Preschoolers* (Illinois: Tyndale, 2004)

4. Oswald Chambers, *My Utmost for His Highest* (Michigan: Oswald Chambers Publications Association, Ltd. 1992)

5. Gary Chapman, *The Five Love Languages* (Chicago: Northfield Publishing, 1992)

6. Joshua Cooley, *Heroes of the Bible Devotional* (Illinois: Tyndale, 2014)

7. Janice Emerson, *The Complete Illustrated Children's Bible* (Oregon: Harvest House, 2014)

8. Gary and Anne Ezzo, *Growing Kids God's Way* (Missouri: Growing Families International, 2007)

9. Willard and Joyce Harley, *Draw Close* (Michigan: Revell, 2011)

10. Dennis and Barbara Rainey, *Moments Together for Couples* (Minnesota: Bethany House, 1995)

11. Zondervan, *The Beginner's Bible* (Michigan: Zondervan, 2005)

12. Filament Bible Experience, https://www.tyndale.com/sites/filamentbibleexperience/

ORDER INFORMATION

REDEMPTION P
PRESS

To order additional copies of this book, please visit
www.redemption-press.com.
Also available at Amazon, Christian bookstores,
and Barnes and Noble.

CPSIA information can be obtained
at www.ICGtesting.com
Printed in the USA
JSHW021327101122
32946JS00001B/79

9 781646 453894